IRMA

A LIGHT IN THE DARK

BY

H.E. POTTER

Contents

COPYRIGHTS

Dedication

If I go down the memory lane and re-live those bittersweet and extremely tough moments; my heart is filled with gratitude for many people. First and foremost, I would like to thank all of my family for their endless work to get me home. I can't imagine what would've happened if it weren't for them. My sincere gratitude to Carnival Cruise and Capt.G. for being there at the right time to rescue me. A lot of things had to go right for the Captain to get me that night. Also, the US coast guard for getting in touch with Carnival and my family.

A special mention to Ms. Wallace at the US Embassy for arranging my emergency passport and keeping my daughters on the right track to bring me home.

This book is dedicated to my good friend and crew, Carl Shephard. I'm sure he's in a better place.

As for me, I've never gone back shrimping ever since. I decided to retire and live in Holiday Florida alone with my cats Shephard and Sadler. I adopted them seven months after losing Motorboat. It's never been easy, but guess that's life; full of surprises.

Prologue

When I was talking to the coast guard, I said we were SW of Ft. Jefferson, 42 nautical miles about 100 miles from Key-West and taking on water. We needed pumps badly. His exact words were; "We have no assets in that area."

Key West had been evacuated. I looked at Carl and said, "It looks like we're on our own." I was checking with the coast guard every half hour. He said they were trying to get in touch with a cruise ship in the area to pick us up. I remember thinking; 'fat chance'.

Even though I kept telling Carl it was going to be okay, I was doubtful. Carl is seventy years old and I didn't want to be the guy who hurts him or crushes his hopes.

I also aimed to have a positive attitude, so I just told Carl that we were going to make it. "Coast Guard is hopeful about getting in contact with the cruise ship, I wouldn't be too worried", I said.

Life as We Know It

I am no stranger to the ups and downs of life. But what do you do when the ebb and flow of life takes the form of a category four hurricane? People talk about grief passing, likening its fluidity to water. But what if you find yourself sinking deeper each day?

I've had a lot on my mind these last few years. My life has never been boring, but these last few years have been exceptional, and not in a good way. I think I actually always wanted the stable, normal life. It just wasn't in the cards for me.

I have three kids – who are now adults. I've been married three times, and unfortunately, none of them lasted – even though I tried my best to make it happen. Even though

I loved the water, it didn't mean my wives loved me on it all the time.

My parents were the best I could've asked for; my siblings and I had a great bond, which I value and appreciate. I could write a book just on the mischief we caused. My mother always made sure even as kids, that my brothers and I had a boat – we're from Florida, and I grew up and spent almost my entire life in Florida. Such is the life, I spent all my time in and around the ocean.

I feel like that influenced me to some extent because now, I'm a shrimper. I've been a shrimper for almost forty-five years, and I love it.

I've spent my entire life at sea, and something about it always felt right. My daughters and I are close, and they love me enough for me to be able to say, that I'm a good dad. So does my son. I'm close to all three of my children; that's one of the greatest joys of life for me. Despite being gone often for work, sometimes months at a time, we've always kept that family bond.

Above all, I aspired to live a simple, honest life. I worked hard all my life to pay the bills. I made sure I provided for whoever I was responsible for, whether it was my kids, my spouse, my parents, my pets, or myself.

I've been married more than once. I was pretty young the first time around, and so was my ex-wife. She was only seventeen at the time, and I met her in high school. I know not a lot of people can say that they married their high school sweetheart, but I always considered myself to be one of the lucky ones to be able to do so.

Unfortunately, it was not the best decision for either of us. Even though we did love each other a lot and we tried to make our marriage work, it didn't work out. We just didn't see eye to eye. And while she's a great person, we felt like we couldn't stay married due to our irreconcilable differences.

I tried to make it work because a part of me was always dedicated to the sanctity of marriage, and I'd always wanted to make my marriage work – we both did.

In the end, we felt like it was time to let go and finally do what's best for our kids, and us. It was a constant struggle, and though we tried our best, it just didn't work, couldn't work that young.

I'm sure I wasn't the only one feeling that way. I mean, you enter a marriage, realizing that you're going to be willfully bound to spend the rest of your life with this particular person – and it'll be everything you wanted and more. You have all these plans and hopes and dreams. Sometimes, they are just dreams.

We were both very disappointed. And just because we decided to not spend the rest of our lives with each other didn't mean we'd be okay without each other. It takes time to let go of a person you were so deeply invested in. It's a great loss, and a person goes through a lot while going through the process.

My children were the best part of my marriage – Marlene, my daughter, and Eddie, my son. They mean the world to me, and I feel like even though our marriage didn't work out, I'd do it all over again for my children.

So, after ten long, tough years filled with differences and confusion, we decided to call it quits and file for divorce. My wife was twenty-seven at the time we got divorced, and I was still young, too, even though I was married for ten years and a father to two children. We were both in high school when married.

We had our entire lives ahead of us, and I'm glad about the decision we took – it was mutual and amicable. Today, I still consider her a great friend, after all, she *is* the mother of my children, and I have a lot of respect for her whenever I realize how great our kids turned out to be. I'm still friendly with her whenever we bump into each other at Grandchildren events. Her, and her now husband, John, who always has some fishing tales to tell. Like the story of him surviving a boat sinking for several days before rescue.

After a while, I met my second wife. This marriage made me happy. I felt as if this time, I got it right. My second wife and I had a daughter together, Jamie. And we moved to Tarpon Springs, Florida. Fishing often has you go where the money in. We moved often but settled in the Tarpon area.

My marriage to my second wife gave me immense hope and strength. It made me feel as if every single struggle that my ex-wife and I went through had been worth it, leading me to this point. What we had was unbelievable. My new wife wasn't too fond of my ex-wife, but my children all got along well.

My children were all happy and healthy, my wife and I were in a great marriage, work was good, my family was all in perfect health, and I was happy.

As I said, life throws something at you when you least expect it. My Father got sick – cancer. And after a long, tiring, and painful battle, he lost his life and left behind me, my brothers and our mother. A battle that was once fought, but came back to fight him again. The second battle, he was unfortunately too old to fight like the first time. We were all devastated by the loss, and I didn't know how to deal with it. Though I was the oldest, I now lived the farthest away. My brother Wesley helped my Mother heal and cope. Which is no small task, given their fifty plus years of marriage.

Before I lost my Father, I'd also lost my Father in Law from my first wife. Billy Mills, who helped me in buying my boat. The boat that helped support three kids and two wives at this point. He really assisted me in getting into the shrimping business. All through high school, I never paid much attention to grades and school. I always knew I was going to be a fisherman like my Dad. Despite being great at football and being MVP my senior year, as were my brothers actually, fishing was all I wanted. Fishing started to become a major stress factor as well though.

Fuel prices started to sky rocket during this time, causing huge financial concerns. So, it's safe to say the happy times had ended. The financial stress caused my wife to go to work to help with health insurance costs, self-employed insurance was getting out of control. She worked part time to get the family coverage and give her some spending money. My youngest daughter was grown up enough to drive herself around so a distance grew between all of us, as my oldest children started their own families. My wife and I of nearly twenty years, separated. It was just another loss of many to come. Then Mom got sick.

My mother, Nona, was so madly in love with my father, Hubert, that after his passing she started having health problems. She started having issues almost immediately. She would sometimes say things like she wanted to be with her husband again. We all worried for her. After a while the mental health turned into the physical health. My brother Wesley being just an hour away tried everything to take care of her. He tried at-home nurses, nursing homes, prescriptions. All that resulted, was a strain on his own marriage from his wonderful wife Terry, being frustrated about how stubborn our mom was. Mom once had her kitchen catch fire and hosed it down with a garden hose herself, claiming the fire department would never get there in time. Around this point, I decided to be a bit stubborn myself and remarried. I was introduced to an old high school girlfriend despite some fire alarms I saw myself. We moved in together and got married pretty quickly.

Getting a little older, with adult children, I thought this marriage wouldn't have some of the strains of the others. I'd later be proven wrong. I was twitter patted though at the time. I was happy to start a new life with someone again. She had several cats and I got Motorboat as my own. She'd go fishing with me and she'd get into all sorts of mischief out there. Fell overboard a couple times, Anthony my crew man jumped over twice to save her. Things were looking up.

Unfortunately, mom got worse, and my brothers and I decided to transfer her to an assisted care facility. To our disappointment, that didn't work either. She kept insisting she didn't need or want any help, and we thought she was better off with us at home. So, we got her discharged from the facility and brought her back home to take care of her. We appointed hospice care because she was now in critical condition.

I thought this is as bad as it would get. I'm a family man so when another family member was lost it hurt me badly. My second cousin Anthony wasn't just a crew member; he was a very dear friend, like a second son. He had been working with me, sometimes staying with us at home for over five years. I wasn't aware of the skeletons he had in his closet, but I wish I had been; perhaps I might've been able to help him. Anthony lost his life to a drug overdose. I didn't know what demons he was fighting – all I knew was that he was a great young man who wouldn't ever hurt anybody, but apparently himself. Being gone for thirty days at a time makes you lose your tolerance to drugs and alcohol. My boat has always been clean and dry. I'd pay for the groceries, but if you wanted cigarettes you had to buy them yourself. No drugs or alcohol ever, even when I use to drink. I wasn't going to support anyone's habit. I think Anthony was still under the impression he had the tolerance of someone on substances every day, the reality was if you're clean for thirty days you can't pick up where you left off.

Antony's death came as quite a shock to me, because I wasn't even aware of all the things that troubled him to such a great extent, I knew he enjoyed the occasional drink, but I never could've imagined that the situation was so terrible.

He was such a great young man. He was a talker and loved music, and those things are sometimes a nuisance on a boat, me being use to the quiet. Anthony though, his stories and music brought us closer. It was sort of an eye-opener for me because I realized how we take life for granted, every single day. I mourned the loss of his death and promised myself I'd live every day to make it count, and I'd never take anything or anyone for granted again. I'll never forget the day of his funeral, there were still somethings missing, but I wanted him to hear this song I knew he'd love. So, I stayed by his casket and played him the song from my phone and talked to him. He always hated being left alone, hated the quiet. I think that's why he was always talking, telling stories and jokes. I asked friends and family to help pick up the flowers and other items missing because I wanted Anthony to have the company.

Anthony's passing was just another reminder of the family I'd lost and the family I was losing. It made me want to try harder for my own family.

One day, while I was out at sea for a rather long trip, I missed call from my brother, followed by a text that said, "Call me." I was still recovering from the loss of Anthony.

My heart dropped. It was ten o' clock in the morning, and I felt my stomach and heart switch places. I picked up the phone and called my brother, already fearing what I was going to hear.

"Mom passed nine o'clock this morning," he said. It was just as I'd suspected. I sat down, and suddenly, my entire world came crashing down. I asked Carl, my new crewman, first mate, and friend, to turn the boat around and head back home. The entire way back, I don't recall what went on in my mind, but I remember being numb. Mindless of my motions.

I didn't know how to think, feel, or behave. Things were awful, and it was like being attacked by one calamity after the other. If I'm completely honest, I didn't even know a human being was capable of handling such loss. It felt like the dominos were all falling at me. I cut my trip short and made it back home for the funeral. It was a beautiful service and Mom finally, got to go back to Dad.

My eldest daughter Marlene was the closest to my mother and father, and I wanted to be there for her in every way possible. She'd just lost her Grandpa's on both sides of her family, and now, she had lost her Grandma.

At the service, Marlene said some beautiful things about her Grandmother. As a father, I was proud of how composed she was. Even though she's an adult now, it was still pretty impressive how she pulled herself together, considering how close she was to her grandparents. I like to think she gets her desire to be close to family from me.

I made sure I spent a lot of time with my daughter, Marlene, because she was going through a lot, and that made my wife jealous, she didn't like anyone else getting attention. Sometime later, Marlene and I were sitting and looking at photos of my parents and family. We were having a father-daughter moment, and I was very happy because Marlene was feeling better. She was sharing fond memories she had with my parents that I didn't even know had happened.

As a father, that's all I want – for my children to be happy. My wife walked in and told me she's going to bed – in a rather harsh tone. I knew something was up. I'd been married enough times to know this wasn't going to end well.

The next day, when I spoke to her – hoping she'd be in a better mood and maybe she'd care enough to share what was up with her, she said nothing. She wanted to be the martyr and wasn't getting enough recognition for it.

I told her I'd be going on a fishing trip soon, and this one would be longer than the previous one because the last one got cut short because of my mother's death. That's when she finally decided to open up to me. She told me she wasn't happy.

And there it was again – another loss for me. I was blindsided by this one because I was under the impression that things were fine. How would you expect a person to react to such news when they're not even aware of something being wrong? I didn't fight what seemed to be inevitable at that point, and I agreed to whatever she said before leaving.

A third marriage and this one, thinking we were both over fifty, we're going to be together forever. Now, over some small pettiness over attention to my daughter, I was looking at a third divorce.

So, I packed up my items when I returned home after the funeral, spoke to a divorce attorney in case, dropped off some personal items at the boat and planned on taking Motorboat with me on my trip as usual.

Jamie and I had bought a house together in Holiday, FL years prior. We lived together for quite a while, and everything was great. It was perfect. It was when Jamie got married, I realized that I missed having someone too. This was shortly after my second marriage ended so I wouldn't be able to move back with her and her husband. I figured my third wife would move back to Key West so I'd live in the townhome we'd bought together until eventually selling it. It was too much house for just me.

I kept thinking I just needed to talk to her more. Figure out what was making her unhappy and how to fix it. I'm usually pretty good at fixing things. I thought it was a void borne out of skepticism because of my previous failed marriages, but I was wrong. Something was bothering me – and it was for all the right reasons. I tried to talk to her, but it wasn't of any use. She just kept denying that anything was wrong.

To me, it just meant that she wasn't ready to talk about it. I thought it was just going to be an argument of some sort, but it turned out to be so much more and so much worse. I had the weather channel on, and they were reporting a hurricane building.

As I sipped on my coffee, I looked at her and smiled and asked her how she slept. Her answer left me gutted. All I wanted with my coffee in the morning was a smile, not the news of my wife cheating on me. The divorce attorney was apparently a good idea.

Waking up to a Missed Alarm, and a Flood

Back on the water I was trying to clear my head. In less than a month my Mom just passed and my marriage ended. My wife, soon-to-be ex-wife had blindsided me just a few days prior, about an affair she was having just as I was getting ready to leave on a long fishing trip.

I thought I'd got it right this time. I was so sure, but I guess I was wrong, again.

Carl and I were out at sea and the waters were relatively clear, despite the talks of a hurricane coming.

On the boat, I was looking forward to getting work done and not let anything come in the way of it. After a couple divorces already, I knew working would take my mind off things. My boat, the only woman who hadn't hurt me yet.

Later in the day, the weather started to look a little rougher. The sky had turned a grey, matching my mood and thoughts. The hurricane wasn't supposed to be coming anywhere near where I was. Hurricane Irma was supposed to take a hard turn North and scrape by the East coast of Florida.

I had spoken to my family a couple days prior. I was originally planning on returning home to Tarpon Springs to avoid the storm. After the news kept reporting it turning towards the other coast, I decided to just stay behind Ft. Jefferson just passed Key West. Common thing for fisherman. The Fort blocked a lot of the winds and waves and there was several of us out there.

When the weather started to get a little worse still, Carl and I drove the boat away from the Fort and further into the Gulf of Mexico. Several other boats decided to do the same. Once out of the reach of the winds, I decided to lay down for a bit since we were out of the worst of it. I had been up for too long trying to make sure we were out of harm's way. I had spoken to Wesley first, told him all was good.

Two hours later, I woke up to an alarm going off. With two in the engine room I figured we might have a little water. When I reached the engine room I realized the first high water alarm failed, it never went off. So instead of a couple inches, I was staring at a couple of feet of water.

As much as I didn't want any of this to happen, it was happening. And whether I liked it or not, I had to accept it. I told myself that panicking will only make things better. I had to pull myself together, for both Carl and I.

I had Motorboat with me. I always took her with me on my fishing trips – she kept me company and I never felt lonely as long as she was around.

With the water in the engine room, if I didn't get it cleared out soon, it'd be inside the cabin. I secured Motorboat in her carrier to make sure I didn't lose track of her. Carl and I assessed the damage.

We were desperately trying to find the source from where all the water was coming from. Carl and I were running around and even though we tried really hard not to panic, it was to no avail. How do you not panic?

Hurricane Irma never took the sharp turn North it was supposed to, causing Key West to evacuate and the storm was getting closer to our location.

We headed to the freezer to check if maybe that's where the water was coming from, nothing. Everywhere we looked, we couldn't get a concrete read on where the water was coming from.

The water level kept getting higher and so did our stress levels. I tried to surround myself with the hope of getting out of this place in one piece, all safe and sound. So, I tried to distract myself as best I could. Happy thoughts to produce a happy outcome.

A while before I went to sleep, we were on the boat talking about the salty wind and how us shrimpers are so used to the waters. For everyone else, fishing is a luxury and something they do for fun. For me, it's how I make a living.

But whenever I think about it, I'm always grateful for being blessed with enough skills to make a good living and provide for myself and my family. Being a shrimper has its pros, and unfortunately, I was about to find out the cons.

The storm never hit us, to this day I can't fathom what exactly happened. We were far from the storm, though it got closer than we wanted. We had outrun the winds when something gave. The high water alarm failed and that just shouldn't happen. It was breaking day when I woke up and began to look for the water source and I only feared it was going to get worse. Daylight meant that if things got worse, we'd at least be able to be seen when he asked for help.

Carl, being older wasn't very capable of climbing the stairs up and down into the engine room. I began working to clear out the pumps. From the water coming in, silt had built up, clogging them. They were chocking. Unable to pump out the water, I found what I thought might be the cause of the water. The stuffing box. I was working to plug it. Carl while in the cabin, was handling the satellite phone. Ironically, I had only purchased the satellite phone a year ago because my Wife had wanted to talk with me when I was out.

Trying to work on the pumps and going back to work on the stuffing box, in a moment of panic and frustration I dropped the tools I was had. They were now buried in several feet of grey silted water. And the water levels kept rising. Without my tools, the little good I was doing was now not possible. It was devastating.

The bigger concern now was the water was only getting higher and Irma still hadn't made a full turn North. It was now heading up the West coast, closer to me, and my children on land.

Over forty years working on the ocean, I've experienced several hurricanes. I've also experience water in the engine room, I've experienced pumps failing. I've experienced all of these things before, just never taking place simultaneously.

When I realized I wasn't going to resolve this myself. I asked Carl to get on with the Coast Guard. Little did we know, they had been evacuated to Miami. They couldn't help. After the storm, sometime the next morning. They might be able to send a helicopter. They informed us, "There are no assets in the area."

The coast guard also informed us about a nearby cruise ship. It was a Carnival Cruise ship and I couldn't imagine them actually helping. The coast guard got us in touch with the cruise ship and we constantly kept updating them about our location. Carl and I split up on the boat, all the while, the water kept rising.

We were 100 miles west of Key West and we were struggling to find a spot to stand without being ankle or some places knee deep in water. The coast guard asked us to abandon the boat and get on the life raft – but, Carl didn't like the idea. Instead, we inflated the life raft and had it tied to the side of the boat.

Attempting to bail out the boat, talk with the Coast Guard, and keep my sanity. It was too much. The anxiety got a hold of me and I started throwing up from the feeling. I was too overwhelmed. I hadn't eaten anything all day and drank just a can of Coke to get some sugar in my system. Just trying to propel myself forward with a can of Coke and stress as motivators.

The heat was unbearable. After a hurricane comes through your left with the thick humidity dragging you down. Things were starting to shut off around the boat as the water claimed more and more territory. Personal possessions of mine were bumping into my legs.

I had a chance to speak to my daughters, brothers and son. They told me to stay afloat. They told me to survive. They each told me something that helped keep me grounded.

The water was coming too quickly though. Carl, who'd been on sinking boats before, was convinced the boat would float for several days. Which is possible, had my boat been wood. My boat was fiberglass. Neither of us really knew what would happen when it took on too much water. My boat being fiberglass had a lot of equipment and cement in it to help stabilize it when the fuel levels were low and we were returning home. Would we have minutes or days? Did these wood boats Carl had been on have the same?

After one last call to the Coast Guard and Carnival Cruise, Carl told me it was time to get in the water. I knew Carl didn't want to get on the raft but I needed him to. When the coast guard asked us if we could swim, Carl didn't answer. I didn't own a cruise ship, my boat wasn't for swimming in the afternoons. We have life rafts and jackets, the question should never have needed to come up.

So, I didn't know whether or not Carl could swim when we were making our way out of the cabin. I grabbed the satellite phone and put it in a Ziploc bag. I grabbed Motorboat and started out the cabin to get to the raft. In this time, I lost Carl. I thought he was right there with me. After all, he had been the one who told me it was time. Running out of the boat, one of the items on my life jacket caught hold of the door frame. I pulled out my pocket knife, cutting it away. Unsure what life saving device on my life jacket I was cutting off. I couldn't think about that though, the water was coming too fast.

Finally free, I stepped out to what was once my deck, now level with the ocean. Usually a good twelve feet in the air. The life raft, tied to the side of the boat caught a wave and it lunged at me. I was held under the water by the thing that's supposed to save me. I couldn't breathe and started to panic. The irony of this being the thing that's going to drown me. I was wedged up against the roof of the cabin, unable to breathe. To get released from the raft, I had to let go of my cat's carrier. I had to sacrifice my little girl that I've had for five years. Motorboat was lost somewhere that night. Lost in the ocean without Anthony to jump in and save her. My glasses were gone and so was the satellite phone. And the worst part is that I didn't even have a single second to process it because every second was precious. The boat was going down very fast and I needed to find Carl and get him into the raft.

We both had our life jackets on but I couldn't find Carl. He was somewhere on the boat but with the lights going out, the wind and waves, I couldn't get sight of him.

I was just a few feet from the raft so I jumped in and swam the short distance. I was looking around for Carl, yelling for him. I pulled out my knife again and began cutting the lines to the boat. The raft was supposed to pull its self free, break away lines, when under too much tension. I couldn't be sure. After the first was cut, the second snapped free on its own.

The boat was going down so quickly and the outriggers and cables we're coming down on me. I had to break free totally. With so many moving parts on the boat now looming over my head, I had to just believe they wouldn't hit the raft and drag me to the bottom. Getting caught up in the rigging was a palpable fear. Once the first two lines were free I lost sight of the outriggers, I don't know which side of me they passed over on their way down because of the dark, but they didn't catch hold of the raft.

I was hopeful that once in the raft, Carl would see me and take the leap. Or I'd be able to catch sight of him finally not fighting for my own life. I caught a glimpse of him running towards the stern of the boat, the opposite direction of the raft. I can only assume he was thinking this was the last high ground and it'd float.

Then the last tension line snapped free, I was spun around. The life raft has a tent and I wasn't facing the boat any longer. Couldn't look for Carl. I heard Carl then cry out, "Captain Eddie! Captain Eddie!" The nose of the boat sunk before I could turn back around. I never did see the letters Capt. Eddie go down.

By the time I could face where the boat was, there was nothing but debris that I couldn't make out in the moon light only. In less than a minute, I had lost my friend, my cat, business and boat.

Some of debris had meaning. Some of the debris was unrecognizable, bits of things I worked around for 38 years but now couldn't make out. The hatch door to the freezer had blown up from the water pressure consuming the engine room and freezer. It floated up and over to the raft, knocking into a few times. With some serious thought, I leaned slightly out of the raft in the high winds and fifteen foot plus seas to shove the hatch door away. The last thing I needed has a hole popped in the thing.

I was floating adrift in the ocean. I felt around the life raft. There were items secured all over the sides. I didn't want to open or remove anything yet. I was going to have to keep my hands and feet unencumbered if I was going to be saved. For over an hour, I was forced to sit there alone, reliving what just happened. The losses were too great. That time alone took my mind to some dark places. I just had to keep hoping I'd be found. Once rescued, maybe I could start to heal with the support of my family. I just needed to make it a little longer.

I didn't know the Captain of the cruise ship had already searched several grids and was still searching. When the cruise ship came into view, it was massive. I'd never been on a cruise ship and from the point of view of a life raft it was relieving and frightening at the same time.

I kept looking at the lights on the ship but I didn't know how I'd get there. The water was very rough and I didn't even know if the Captain on the ship could have the life boats lowered down because the water and the winds were still so severe. I also didn't know if they could see me. I was just a speck compared to this massive ship.

On top of the life raft was a small blinking light. Lucky for me, the Captain did see it. They were on their way to me. The item I had cut away from my life jacket earlier, wasn't my strobe light. I began blinking SOS to the cruise ship, praying these little lights were enough.

I'd spoken to my daughter earlier when the storm had started to close in and all of a sudden, I remembered what she'd said. After I explained the situation to her, she said; "Dad, don't you go down with that boat. I mean it, do not go down with that boat – you have got to make it through this."

My daughter's words echoed in my head and they gave me more than enough strength to make it through. I know that just remembering her words in that moment gave me the strength I needed. I didn't know how much more strength I was going to need, apparently it was going to be a lot.

I knew that the cruise ship was very high and that due to the weather conditions, it'd be impossible for them to lower their lifeboats at this point. I didn't know if there were any other ways but all I knew then was that I really had to make it to that ship – my life entirely depended on it.

My raft surfed over to the cruise ship and I waited at the bottom of the ship for them to figure out a way to get me there. The ship had these search lights and they pointed right into the water. It was still so dark, but the lights from the ship were so bright. They found me.

The captain was quite a man; I'll never forget him. He told me they couldn't lower the lifeboats because it'd be useless due to the situation of the water and the winds – it's be too much of a risk. So, he turned the ship sideways to block the wind from the other direction and he lowered down a ladder. Getting a ship that size to hold a position in those winds, he was full throttle to block as much from me as possible. He was maneuvering an 855 foot ship to keep me alive. Then it was my job to save myself, I had to get to the ladder.

The ladder seemed to be a hundred miles away from the life raft because of the waves. The raft would jump up from a wave and I'd get close but the wind would blow the ladder away. When the waves took the raft it was nearly impossible to keep my footing as I was thrown around and the raft lurched and lunged. Debris from my boat was still around me, a boot bobbed up and down with me saying its last goodbye.

I felt like I didn't ever want to give up on this fight for survival but it just kept getting more challenging. I tried to reach out for the ladder several times but it did no good. I couldn't reach that long and I kept fearing I was going to fall into the water. Up against the cruise ship with those engines going, the water was not where I wanted to be.

One of the officers on the boat yelled out something I'd never forget. I still hold his words so close to me in my heart. He said;

"Dig deep in your heart and find the strength to grab on to that ladder, you can do it!"

Those words were all I needed to hear apparently. I instantly thought about my daughters and my son and the strength appeared as if out of nowhere. I tried again to reach out to the ladder. And this time, the water came up just enough to get me to the level of the bottom of the ladder. For once this day, the high seas were a blessing.

I caught on with all my strength. I had twenty feet or so to climb in these awful conditions. The crew were helping pull me up but they couldn't do it all themselves. I had to climb. My arms shook with the effort. The waves were still reaching out to my feet, trying to get me back. The exhaustion from the day, lack of food and energy weren't helping my case. I took one rope ladder rung at a time, with a crew of men helping with each once of effort I put in. As soon as I'd realized I was in a safe place, my body gave in. I collapsed and the kind gentlemen put me on a wheelchair and took me to an infirmary to get me treated.

There was at first a lot of panic and fear from the crew, they thought Carl was in the raft with me and was lost off the ladder. I had to explain to them, Carl didn't make it off the boat.

I was severely dehydrated, I had trouble breathing. The Captain told me I was still in shock and I didn't have to know anything from a medical perspective to know he right he was.

I couldn't imagine what I had just survived and I couldn't imagine Carl and Motorboat not being with me. Now that I could finally rest, the sad reality kicked in. I lost two living beings and one of my prized possessions; Captain Eddie – my boat.

Survival Suit vs. Survival Jacket

Each second that passed, got tougher and tougher. And somehow, I felt as if I was losing the strength to stay strong and keep the faith. I had sustained a few minor injuries but it's the stress and the anxiety which kept growing on me. I had just witnessed two deaths and I didn't even know if I was safe yet.

I was asked to rest as soon as I got on board the carnival. The kind people on the ship got me checked out at the infirmary as quick as possible but the best thing for me was rest.

How could I rest when I've never felt this restless in my entire life? Despite being in one of the most difficult situations of my life, all I could think about were my kids. How they would've been frantic and in absolute panic trying to get a hold of me.

So, I asked the captain and requested him to please find a way that'd help me speak to my kids. The captain then informed me that they'd already gotten in touch with the coast guard and they've been informed that I made it safely onto the Carnival. There's one sigh of relief I remember breathing during all of this. It was nearly the only one.

So I followed orders. They kept a very tight ship with someone outside my room at all times. I wondered if it was a suicide watch. They tried to feed me and make me comfortable but I had too much misery growing in my gut. I didn't have a phone, a book, a computer, my cat, my boat, my family. Nothing that was usually an escape of these negative feelings. I guess to follow some routine I took a few showers. I'd get up and shower. I'd try to lay down but everything I wanted to push out of my mind kept flooding in. So, I'd get up and take another shower. I remembered the memories that I didn't want to remember. In fact, the ones I'd do anything to forget. Even in the state of panic, my mind wandered off to the events of my life that I didn't want to.

I remembered losing Carl and Motorboat a few hours ago, which quickly led me to remembering losing my parents, ex-Father in law and Anthony. I didn't want to remember this, all I needed right now was to feel better. So, I tried to divert my mind.

This time, I thought about something so much more unconventional. I thought about how on my way here, I'd just offered my soon to be ex wife and her new boyfriend, a place in my home – while I'd be gone.

It wasn't my best moment, that's for sure. But it really got me thinking. I have absolutely no clue why I even thought of something of that sort. I guess bad things just happen. Maybe God intended to test all the strength I have because I can say one thing is for sure; I've been getting testing *a lot* lately. It's like each day there's a trivial or major situation just waiting for me when I wake up.

Everyone back home would've been evacuated by now and everyone should be safe and sound. I was hoping my kids were okay. I couldn't stop thinking about them – no matter how much I tried not to. What if I could've saved Carl? Maybe part of me should've known that he couldn't swim. A million thoughts constantly clouded my mind.

I felt like I needed to speak to the Captain and get an update about our current situation and our action plan from here on out. So, I decided to leave the infirmary and find the Captain. I was a nervous wreck and I needed air.

After speaking to the Captain, I learned that we were headed for Freeport, Bahamas. Just because they picked up a straggler on the way, didn't mean they were dropping me off at home. The ship was headed to the Bahamas because it was in the middle of renovations when Irma first arrived. They had evacuated the Bahamas and now were just, heading back. With me as a carry on.

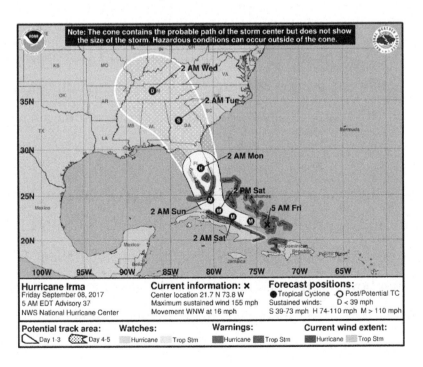

After speaking to the Capt. I at least knew where I was headed. I was able to think clearer. I was glad we were headed to a safe zone. And for now, I was just lucky to be alive. I didn't know how long we'd take to get there – given the weather conditions and all. But I knew that all that mattered to me for now was, being alive.

I didn't know this at that moment but the whole time, my daughters and my son had been in touch with the Captain and the Coast Guard. They kept requesting constant updates about me and my surroundings. They even went on to ask about Carl and Motorboat – whether or not they'd made it. Just so they'd understand my condition (mental and physical) better.

It took about two nights to get to Freeport. I didn't exactly know how to get back home because I had lost all of my belongings and I knew for a fact that once we reached shore, I'd need help. I didn't know necessarily how to get the help. I currently had no money, no identification, was arriving in a foreign country. I was given some reading glasses but couldn't really see. I was wearing sweatpants and a dirty t-shirt. I was apparently going to need a lot of help.

My brother was back in Raleigh, North Carolina and I had spoken to him on the satellite phone before the boat went down. Even though I was going through possibly the worst thing to ever happen to me, I couldn't help but think what my family must've been going through.

They were all keeping a check of me and worried sick about me. But I couldn't talk to them. I didn't have the access or the resources to try. I also didn't know if I had the words yet to verbalize what I just experienced. I was dreading having to have those talks.

My brother at the beginning of the storm had spoken to me, had known I was okay, making the right decision, then everything went wrong. Wesley thought he'd never see me again. Thought he was losing his big brother. He called his son Andrew who said, "Dad, God can move mountains. You've got to have faith in Him". And that's exactly what happened. I had just jumped off a mountain, my boat, into a mountain of waves just to have a cruise ship move into my view to save me. The cruise ship, from a tiny raft in the ocean, is indeed a mountain.

Unsurprisingly, Carnival and its people had quite a process for people like me. They seemed to be prepared for everything. I was assigned an agent to help out with all the documentation and formalities. This agent's job was to ensure that I returned safely when at Freeport.

So, I get assigned an agent on what I remember was either the third or fourth day of rescue. They drove me to an airport where they were setting up a small flight to travel from Freeport to Nassau. Waiting there with the agent, my daughter Marlene called and asked if my flight back to Florida had been covered. I didn't know. I started crying talking to her, just hearing her voice and knowing my daughter was helping bring me home. She had to ask me a bunch of questions for my ticket. The phone call with my daughter was a rather emotional one. I was bawling like a little girl when she asked me about the flight. I had just gone through a lot. So far in this emotional journey, I realized I hadn't been handling it all that well.

So, it's safe to say that my mental state wasn't the best at that very moment. I didn't want to worry my daughter because I was sure she'd already been through enough – not knowing whether or not her father would return from this nightmare. I heard her tell me;

"Don't worry about this dad. I'm going to take care of this for you."

My daughter, just like the other two children of mine, were everything to me. I knew the hard part was over and all that's left is for me to get on a plane, fly out to Tampa and hug my kids.

I landed in Nassau and met with another agent who took care of things from there. My agent took me to get a passport photo taken. Still wearing a dingy white t-shirt and borrowed reading glasses, I went to a store that took my photo. I was ready to head to the embassy.

Because I had taken an international trip about six months prior, I was already on file. When I got to the Embassy, I met Ms. Wallace. She was in-charge of the emergency cases assigned for return.

Even though I'd just gotten there, I could tell this was the woman for the job. She was running the show. I'm glad she was one of the incredible people helping me get home. She had so much strength and confidence in what she was doing, it kept me grounded. This whole time in the Bahamas I was being shuffled around from one place to the next. I was completely out of my element, but I had a lot of professionals and I was trusting them.

Ms. Wallace asked me to identify a photo of me but I lost my glasses on the boat. The only thing I had were my reader glasses. So, I asked her to give me a minute as I put them on and I said;

"Yes ma'am that is me".

Once she had identified me, we could finally get the process started. She told me I'd be needing an emergency passport to get back to America. Which is why we needed to get started on that immediately. The emergency passport was ready in a couple of hours. Things were off to a good start.

Since I didn't have a dime to my name, my brother Wesley with the help of his son Andrew, sent money to the Embassy. They wouldn't take a wire for some reason, so Andrew figured out how to use Western Union to send me $500. That was covering my flight to Nassau, my passport and my photo.

The process was going to take more than a day which is why I was asked to go check in to a hotel for the rest of the day. Barbara Wallace had recommended to me I go buy myself some dinner and new clothes since there was still a little money left over from what my brother had sent. It was raining when I went to leave, I asked someone if I could get a bag for my passport and personal affects. At this moment, my personal affects consisted of a small amount of money, my emergency passport, my watch and a pocket knife. I was handed a trash bag, at least it kept my things dry. I went over to McDonald's and got myself a hot meal. I hadn't eaten much in days.

I took Barbara's advice and stopped into a gift shop nearby to get myself a clean shirt and shorts. I wasn't able to find any socks but some clean clothes seemed to help.

The Bahamas was actually in quite disarray having just been hit by Irma themselves. Many stores still had standing water in them, sand bags out, and some had sand drifts up against them where the water had pushed it up to the buildings store fronts. The agents were done for the night so I was walking around Nassau on foot. Luckily the hotel and McDonald's where right across the street from the Embassy. I was afraid to walk too far and lose sight of the Embassy.

With some food and clothes, I went straight to the hotel to get some rest and hopefully find the mental peace to get some sleep. I got to the Hilton in Nassau, which was the hotel they'd recommended me to stay at. I got there and I was supposed to have a room booked, but it was booked, just not paid for.

I had spoken to my younger daughter Jamie and she'd told me everything was taken care of. But when I got to the hotel, there was no such arrangement, unfortunately. So, I had to call someone and get an update on where I'd be staying.

Apparently, my daughter's card declined for the international transaction. So, they couldn't charge for the room.

I asked the hotel if there was a phone that I could use to call my brother and ask him to help out with what to do in this situation. As luck would have it, that wasn't possible either. I needed to make an international phone call but I didn't have enough money for the room and there was no room for me to charge the call too yet.

I didn't know the next thing to do. I was under the impression I was just going to walk in and get a key. Luckily, my agent had stopped by there and left his card at the reception in case a slip-up of this sort was to happen – which it did. The receptionist called my agent and informed him of the situation and he gave the receptionist a message for me.

"Please tell Mr. Potter I'll be there in about twenty minutes."

I waited for him to get to the hotel lobby. When he arrived, he asked, "You need a phone?" I explained the mix up and he handed me his phone. I needed a place to stay over night as my flight wasn't until the next morning and the Embassy was now closed.

I used his phone to call my brother and have the entire situation sorted. Which it did within minutes of my brother speaking to the receptionist. I handed the phone back to my agent and thanked him. He double checked all the necessary arrangements for the next day and arranged a room at the hotel for me to spend the night.

God bless my family for all the help they've been sending my way. God knows if I had to take matters into my own hands at that moment, I'd be in a very difficult position because all I had right then were my chicken nuggets and my emergency passport. I don't know if I had the mental capacity to handle much of this on my own, I guess that's why they assigned me the agents.

The next day, as I was going to the airport – on my way to finally be home, I realized I couldn't be happier. This was happening, finally. I got to the airport and while I was going through customs, the guy checking my passport asks me;

"What constitutes an emergency passport?"

And I ended up telling him everything. Looking back, I realize that he might've been looking for a simpler answer, but I just went all out. I told him about my boat sinking, about being in the middle of a hurricane, about motorboat and Carl and basically everything else I could've remembered in that moment.

The man was pretty impressed and he offered his condolences. And I was finally cleared through customs. I couldn't contain my excitement and part of me felt like I still hadn't processed everything that was happening to me all these days. I still hadn't gotten a chance to catch my breath and feel safe.

I hadn't gotten the chance to grieve the loss of Carl or motorboat either. And I hadn't gotten a chance to fully come back from the state of shock I was in. I was excited to meet my kids and my brothers.

Unfortunately, though, I accidentally told my wife what time I'd be landing at the airport. My wife, soon to be ex-wife wanted to come see me at the airport and maybe because of everything that had happened in the past few days, I forgot that we were separated and that she was with someone else now.

Sometimes that'll happen in a marriage or with basically anyone you're familiar with. Despite going through a hard time, in a state of shock, you'll tend to rely on the positive aspects of the relationship. Maybe because you're in such an awful place and you naturally expect comfort from the people you've been familiar with. Or the ones that are close to you.

I knew one thing for sure. Even though she was being very nice to me, I wanted nothing to do with her. So, even though I made an honest mistake of telling her what time I'd be landing in Tampa, I had absolutely no interest in seeing her. Because, the last time I saw her, she told me she'd be leaving me for someone else.

No matter what storm you ride out, that is one of the many cruel things in life that'll just stay with you, unfortunately.

Thank God for Family

The next day, as I was going to the airport – on my way to finally be home, I realized I couldn't be happier.

This was happening, finally.

Looking back, I realize that he might've been looking for a simpler answer, but I just went all out. I told him about my boat sinking, about being in the middle of a hurricane, about motorboat and Carl and basically everything else I could've remembered at that moment.

The man was pretty impressed, and he offered his condolences. And I was finally cleared through customs. I couldn't contain my excitement, and part of me felt like I still hadn't processed everything that was happening to me all these days. I still hadn't gotten a chance to catch my breath and feel safe.

I hadn't gotten the chance to grieve the loss of Carl or Motorboat either. And I hadn't gotten a chance to fully come back from the state of shock I was in. I was excited to meet my kids and my brothers.

Unfortunately, though, I accidentally told my wife what time I'd be landing at the airport. My wife, soon to be ex-wife wanted to come to see me at the airport and maybe because of everything that had happened in the past few days, I forgot that we were separated and that she was with someone else now.

Sometimes that'll happen in a marriage or with basically anyone you're familiar with. Despite going through a hard time, in a state of shock, you'll tend to rely on the positive aspects of the relationship. Maybe because you're in such an awful place, and you naturally expect comfort from the people you've been familiar with. Or the ones that are close to you.

I knew one thing for sure. Even though she was being very nice to me, I wanted nothing to do with her. So, even though I made an honest mistake of telling her what time I'd be landing in Tampa, I had absolutely no interest in seeing her. Because the last time I saw her, she told me she'd be leaving me for someone else.

No matter what storm you ride out, that is one of the many cruel things in life that'll just stay with you, unfortunately.

While I was waiting for my flight updates at the airport, I decided to distract myself, so I wouldn't think of stuff I wanted to avoid right now. I started to think about my family. I kept thinking about how I couldn't be anywhere if it wasn't for my family.

I recalled how my daughters had constantly kept calling and trying their best to stay in touch with the captain to ask about me. After everything I'd been through these past couple of days, I couldn't help but think how blessed I am.

I've had a pretty good life, despite the series of unfortunate events that happened to me time after time. I've had the opportunity to fall in love and make great memories.

Most people aren't lucky enough to have such strong ties with their family, but I consider myself one of the lucky ones. Mainly because of my relationship with my children and also my siblings.

When my parents were alive, all three of us (my brothers and I) would make it a habit to go see our parents regularly. The thought of them having to do anything alone was devastating. Besides, I've always felt like it's always old age when parents need their children the most.

I'm not exactly in the prime of my youth right now, but when I think about my relationship with my family, I feel content. They're always there when I need them and even when I don't.

Not many people can say that, which is why I honestly cherish my life and my relationships. My children have always been my biggest support system. I'd like to think I really got it right as their dad, or that I must've done something right in life when I decided to raise them the way I did.

They make me proud. I see three of the most beautiful human beings, inside out, with exceptional morals and values, and I don't mean to take credit for any of their attributes, but I can surely say that it fills my heart with joy.

Maybe it's because I've seen what's out there. I don't mean to brag, but a lot of my friends my age don't have the same relationship with their kids as I do. This makes me sad because every parent should have a special bond with their child.

I've always given family great value and importance in life; maybe that's why I somehow managed to keep my family so close to me.

Well, whatever it is, I'm just glad that I was able to make things work. It's testing time like these that really make me count my blessings. We as people tend to make it habit to not appreciate the little things in life. And I mean, why would we? When we've been blessed to get everything we've ever wanted and everything we've ever needed, we lose sight of the value it holds.

Just like I almost did. I never really ever lost sight of what was important to me – family, but I didn't appreciate it the way I do now either. Which brings me back to my point. We always only realize the true value of something when we're without it.

The situation that I'm remembering reminds me how bad I wanted to hug my kids at that moment. Being away from them and not knowing whether or not I'd get to see them again was misery on its own. I missed my children, and even though they're all grownups and busy in their own lives, I couldn't imagine a life where they wouldn't have their dad.

I know this because I lost my dad not too long ago, and my mother a while after; it was devastating, to say the least.

My parents always made sure that my brothers and I had a very nice childhood. They brought us up with a lot of love, and at the same time, discipline. Our parents instilled all the values that they held very close to their hearts. And for that, I thank them every day.

My brothers and I had always been like friends. It was an awesome experience getting to grow up with not one but two brothers. It was fun, it was challenging, and it was something I'll always cherish.

Even today, the relationship that my brothers and I share is something I value a lot. My brothers Wesley and Kevin were worried sick when I was on that boat and caught up in the storm.

Even in an entirely different country, they ensured that I had everything I needed – no matter how during the storm. Their efforts to guarantee my safe return were evident, and the more I think about it, the more I want them to know how much they mean to me.

Even though what I went through was absolutely terrible, it would've been a lot worse if it wasn't for my children, my brothers, and everyone else who helped me through this difficult process.

I mean, could you imagine the stress of having to find accommodation and trying to figure out a way to get back home without having anything to your name? Not even something as little as an ID or my cell phone. And yet, they somehow made it work.

I am, sitting at the airport after enduring one of the worst hurricanes the country has seen in a while. And I have the convenience of returning back home safely, despite having lost everything in the storm.

Times like these make you realize the true value of material things – it barely amounts to anything when you've got your family by your side. That's all that really matters.

I didn't know how the situation was going to be when I'd get back. I knew the storm had hit Florida too; I just didn't know how much damage there'd be for me to see.

Luckily, no one told me to worry about that. Nobody even talked about our house or what condition it was in. fortunately, there was no damage. But even if there was, I wouldn't really care for it. At least I think I wouldn't. Neither would my family. Because as far as my understanding goes, they were beyond overjoyed to see me come back home – in one piece.

I still think it was a great loss that we lost Carl and Motorboat, and I wish there was something I could've done to help avoid the tragedy but sadly, nothing was in my hands at that moment.

In fact, the likelihood of me being alive was little to none, and I somehow made it. I could never forget the moment when the captain asked me to jump on the ship with all my strength. It was pitch dark, the tides were so high, and the water was as unsteady as a running river.

The size of the waves crashing into one another was unimaginable. I can't help but think I would've definitely been swept away by one of those.

But divine intervention was what that was. I am a man of faith, and I believe that God always works out a way for us. The fact that I had the strength to make it on to that boat was God's way of showing me my path. I knew my time couldn't be up.

I knew that God had so much more in store for me, and this couldn't be it. However, every time I saw a giant wave come crashing by, I'd think otherwise. But then again, my only explanation for the reason I'm alive is God's help.

Otherwise, there could've been no way anyone would've made it through a storm that severe. Honestly, that's all I needed. Because, here I am – alive and kicking. I couldn't have asked for anything more, and even though I'm hours away from going home, I can't help but think about how my kids must be feeling right now.

I knew I was very close to hugging them and holding them and making them believe that their dad was okay, but I just couldn't seem to get that thought out of my mind.

Everything happens for a reason, and there's always a bright side for every unfortunate situation. These are the two lessons I've learned in life. They're also the lessons which have taught me a lot in life.

From teaching me how to be a good father and finding comfort in the fact that a shrimper is what I'm supposed to be, these lessons have taught me everything there is to know about life.

Everything happens for a reason; this is something that's become very popular with people who are deemed unrealistic. Unfortunately, that's not the case at all. People tend to believe that this is an excuse that optimists use when something ill-fated happens to them.

For me, it was the exact opposite and served an entirely different purpose. Everything happens for a reason, not because we're trying to justify that something unfortunate happened to us, but because we believe that something much better is coming our way.

This is where your faith plays a huge part in your life. It alters your perspective and paves the way for what you believe in. So, for me, it was always about being optimistic and having complete faith in the higher power. God's plan isn't just a phrase to me; it's a real thing.

As far as the other lesson is concerned, that's a tricky one. Sometimes in life, we're placed in a situation so bad that our only option is to give up. But, that's not even an option for most of us. And it shouldn't be for the rest of us either.

I know it's difficult, and it seems very unreasonable to try and think of something positive out of something that can possibly alter your whole life. But in life, there are several things that we hear in our daily lives, which are much more than just a sentence. If we ever dig a little deeper and truly understand their meaning, we wouldn't need help understanding ourselves.

For instance, when life gives you lemons, you make lemonade. While this metaphor might seem quirky and hilarious, it's so much more than just a sentence to casually slide into a pep-talk.

It basically translates to "If life keeps throwing unfortunate circumstances at you, you've got to make something out of it."

Even if it's the tiniest of efforts – it's the thought that counts. And eventually, it's the positive thoughts that help you make it through the tough times. Having something to look forward to and believing in something is a different kind of strength, believe me.

When I was seconds away from potentially drowning to my death, I held on tight to what was important to me – my family. The memories we'd made together made me strong enough to conquer the world. And I know most people just say that, but the strength that I'm referring to in this context is the strength that comes from within.

Looking forward to something gives you the strength to fight harder. This doesn't only apply to sinking boats, cheating wives, and hurricanes. In fact, it applies to any and every awful situation in life.

Whenever you're stuck in a place that you feel like you can't get out of, picture a happy memory or a goal that you're very driven toward but are yet to accomplish. The strength will appear as if from out of nowhere.

That's what it really means to always look on the brighter side of things. And most importantly, in my age, I've realized a very important and valuable life-hack of some sort. Nothing ever really goes to waste as long as you make something out of it. As long as you're focused on the bigger picture, the unfortunate situation in the present will seem like nothing to you.

For me, enduring the hurricane was hell. I had to witness my shrimping partner lose his life in front of my very eyes in a split second. I lost my beloved pet. I lost my boat; these losses weren't just any ordinary losses. They took a toll on me and my mental health, but I made it out. All because I focused on the bigger picture and focused on the brighter side of things.

I know it's insane to even think there'd be a bright side to all this, but there actually was. First off, the odds of me surviving the storm were little to none. If it hadn't been for the Carnival, I wouldn't have been saved. And for that ship to just happen to make its way back passing me? Like I said, it was divine intervention.

Surviving that hurricane made me believe that my life is worth something more than I imagined. I've lived a pretty great life, and I've lived long enough to see my kids grow up into the most beautiful people ever. Some would even say that I've done it all and seen it all.

Yet, God found a way to keep me alive. Which clearly means I have a greater purpose in life. And having survived one of the worst moments of my life has helped me realize and find my strength. Being a survivor is one of the best things to ever happen to me.

Living to tell the tale isn't just a metaphor for me anymore; it's real life. And one day, I'll be telling this very story to my grandkids, and I'll watch their faces light up with joy as I teach them everything I've learned. Especially that you're supposed to find everything you'll ever need – within yourself.

The storm was the worst thing to ever happen to me, in line with all the other unfortunate instances that occurred this year. All the people close to me that I lost and my wife's betrayal. Tough times differ and vary from person to person. Knowing how to make it through is what's important.

So, there I was, all set to head back home after hours of gratitude and evaluation. I knew the hard part was over but what I was really dreading was the other hard part, having to face my soon-to-be ex-wife. I don't even remember why I shared my arrival details with her.

I was so certain that no part of me wanted her there. All I wanted were my kids and my brothers. I guess I was really overwhelmed when I spoke to her on the phone. And the worst part is that we left things on such a bad note, I was so confused about how I should react when I see her.

Obviously, she was expressing a lot of concern for me, but that still didn't help me figure out how to behave with her. What she did was unforgivable, and I know for a fact that there was no coming back from it.

Nevertheless, I was about to find out. I still had a couple of hours before I head back home, and this was one thing I wanted to not think about at all, but unfortunately, my mind somehow got around to it.

Coffee in the morning, and adultery

All that thought about not knowing how to react to when I see her got me wondering about where exactly I stand with her. I knew for a fact that I wasn't going to stay married to her, but at the same time, I couldn't help but think about where we'd pick up from after I got back.

I've been married long enough to know how marriage works. I've been married enough times to know the amount of dedication, devotion, and compromise it takes to *stay* married. Love is a tricky thing. A person in love is believed to behave a certain way. There are this newfound optimism and hope in almost everything you do once you're in love.

Of course, everything is great at first, but then after a while, it gets tough and tricky. There's no sure shot way of knowing whether or not someone will end up being the right person for you. You can try a million different things with a million different people, but nothing in this world can guarantee the success of your marriage except consistent efforts from both parties.

The second you begin to get tired of making efforts for your significant other is when things start to go south. People joke about the charm of marriage wearing off after a while, whereas I don't think that should ever happen in a marriage.

Everyone needs companionship in this world. God created us in pairs for a reason – so that we always have someone to have and to hold. Whether it's a human being or an animal, the entire purpose of life, in some way or another, is to be with the person you're meant to be. And I know this for a fact, none of us were made to be alone. No matter how bad things might seem for a particular period, I don't believe we should ever give up hope when it comes to finding your soulmate.

The difficult thing is that there's no time for any of us to meet the right person. Which tends to make people anxious. The waiting is what gets to them, and they begin to feel like if it isn't going to happen any time soon, it probably won't ever happen for them – at all. Believing this is what leads many of us into a rushed decision.

I don't blame anyone. I know how difficult it can be to be without someone. Especially after you reach that certain age in life where you don't have much to do – you begin to crave companionship. If I can say anything from the experiences I learned in my marriage, everything happens for a reason. I believe that because God led me to believe that.

No time or efforts of yours can go to waste because sooner or later, you'll realize that everything that happened to you worked out for the best – God's plan! Even though it might seem like the world is ending, and believe me, I know the feeling. After investing a lot of time in someone, building your entire life around someone, when things don't go as planned, it hurts, and you feel as if all your efforts went in vain.

From all of my three marriages, I learned to never regret something that has already happened and was inevitable, to begin with. If you get married, there's always a possibility of things working out if one of the two partners begin to see things differently. Like I said, there's no telling what is going to make your marriage work and what isn't. it all depends on a person's own efforts.

For me, marriage always a huge milestone for me. I've always believed it completes who you are as a person. My first marriage taught me that it doesn't always work out. No matter how likely it might seem, things tend to change after a while, and not everyone has the patience to deal with that.

There are always second chances, or in my case, there were more than three. The first time was the time I felt that I got it right. I gave it my all; it was a dream come true for me. I believe that we both made efforts to keep the marriage afloat, but somewhere, somehow, one of us lacked. One of us or both of us just decided that we'd be better off apart than we would, together.

The same thing happened the second time around. Somehow, somewhere with time, we grew apart. And that's okay. I'm old enough, and I've lived life enough to know that nothing works out as you expect it to. Barely ever.

When I gave up on love again and decided to live with my daughter for a while, things were good. I got to spend time with my daughter, and we formed a close connection. Not that we didn't have one already, but it's always a great thing for me to spend time with my kids. I was by myself for a while, and I enjoyed it. I enjoyed making time for things I hadn't done for ages. I practiced self-care and looked after my cats. They meant a lot to me. Especially Motorboat, who I lost during the hurricane.

So, now that I'm about to see my soon to be ex-wife again, it's bringing up a whole bunch of feelings I didn't know I felt. And unfortunately, despite my constant efforts, it keeps taking me back to the morning that I found out about her affair. It was so casual for her like it didn't even mean anything to her. But for me, my entire world came crashing down.

I think it's safe to say by now that I don't have a hard time dealing with loss because of how used to it I am. I don't have a hard time dealing with loss because of the series of unfortunate events that life kept presenting to me – one after the other.

That being said, I think that in a way, those circumstances make you value the little things in life and really appreciate something good when you finally get it. That was the case with my soon to be ex-wife.

I felt that the worst was gone and that nothing could go wrong anymore. After all, a lot of bad had happened, and I didn't expect so many tests from God. Not in such a short time, at least. I thought this marriage of mine was going to stick. Not because I did everything right. But because I didn't believe in that much bad luck or something unfortunate happening to one person.

It was a beautiful morning. I remember it like it was yesterday – unfortunately. I woke up in the morning and made coffee for her and for me. Something felt off. I couldn't put my finger on it, though. This was my wife, and I knew something was wrong. But boy, did I guess it wrong. According to my, it could've been something I might've said or something I'd forgotten to do at most.

But I was literally in shock after what I heard. My wife of over five years told me that she wanted a divorce. Again, I was under the impression that everything was alright, and it could've been a misunderstanding at most. Nothing major or severe.

I was blindsided. I am drinking my coffee, enjoying the beautiful morning, and someone just decided to throw something so major at me. I was in utter shock, but I somehow gathered the courage to ask her, "why?".

To my dismay, it wasn't something as basic or mundane as 'we grew apart' or 'she just doesn't love me anymore.' My wife was having an affair. And to make everything worse, she walked up to me in broad daylight and confessed her feelings while I was drinking my morning coffee. It was awful. I felt my heart sink, and I felt broken.

I felt as if something had been taken away from me again. Another loss. This was my time to get it right; I'd already failed twice before. If this didn't work, what would? I was in utter shock, but I told her 'okay.' I honestly did not know how else to respond. I didn't know what to do at that moment. I couldn't understand whether I should use my energy to process what she just sprung at me or respond to her.

So, I said okay, and I finished my coffee, and I left. From the looks of it, she was pretty surprised too. Because she didn't seem to handle my reaction (or the lack of it) all too well. I had to go on my shrimping trip, and I had to get moving fast because I remember the storm was closing in, according to the forecast.

After I left, that was the last I saw of her or spoke to her face to face. And now, it's killing me and bothering me so much – I don't know what to do or how to react when I see her at the airport. Is she going to want to hug me? Is she going to want to kiss me? Is she going to apologize and take everything back because of everything that happened after?

I'm dreading seeing her, but right now, all I wanted to focus on was getting home. I convinced myself constantly that I had just survived worse and that nothing could compare to whatever I had gone through in the past few days. I fought death, and I was on my way back home. If God put me in such difficult situations, he sure got me out of them too.

So, my strategy here was to only focus on the positive side. Because if I compared anything, any amount of negative or misfortune to the positive side, it would amount to nothing. And I am truly grateful for that. I knew I didn't want to be with her, though. That much I was sure of.

And that's because I had already made my peace with the fact that she and I were done. In fact, before I left, and before everything happened, she told me the same morning that she'd be moving out of my house and into her new boyfriend's house in Marathon, within a week. To which again, I didn't say anything.

When the storm was closing in, and all my family members were evacuating all the areas we lived in, which were predicted to get hit by the flood, I even offered her to stay in our house until I got back.

I didn't just offer her to stay. I offered her to stay with her boyfriend. To which again, she was very surprised and asked me several times if I was entirely sure of what I was saying – I was. I didn't want anything to do with her. And the fact that she already had someone else already made things easier.

It made our process of separation a lot easier to deal with and accept. Because part of me felt that – this way, I didn't have to work to save anything. Because there was absolutely nothing left to be saved.

I didn't know what I was going to do about this once I got home. I didn't exactly know how well I'd deal with this either. Maybe part of the reason that I hadn't displayed any sort of emotion or reaction to the whole situation was that I hadn't even begun to process it yet.

I didn't have any kids with her, though. Not that it would change anything, but it just meant that to me, once this marriage ends, there's be absolutely nothing tying us to each other. I have a friendly relationship with my ex-wives, and we've been co-parenting in recent times for as long as I can remember. And it's been working out great.

I believe that a child needs both parents to live life to the fullest. My parents had always been such great parents. They really set an example for the type of marriage my siblings and I should all have one day. Which is why I always looked up to my parents' marriage. I never wanted to fail at it – but I guess that sometimes, life has other plans for you.

My parents' marriage was a fairytale. They were married for 53 years, and I can honestly say that those 53 years were the best of their lives. They set an excellent example for us. My parents were head over heels in love. I'd never seen two people so right for each other. Everything that I learned about love and marriage came from looking at those two.

Even before my dad died, they'd sit and talk for hours and just drink their coffee or take a walk sometimes. They were each other's world, and I'd never seen it any other way for as long as I can remember. After my dad died, my mom's world came crashing down. My mother was an amazing woman.

She was a great wife, very caring, and very loving. She kept my dad the happiest he'd ever been. I'd always seen her very well-dressed, and the way that she always treated my father gave me all the faith I needed to believe in a successful marriage. They would laugh and joke and tease each other. My father was a great husband too. Even after all these years of marriage, he somehow still always made her laugh.

It's like he was always making her fall in love with him – over and over again. When I think about them, my heart fills with joy for the absolutely perfect life that they had. They got to see their kids grow up and build their own lives, they got to see their grandkids.

It makes me very happy that my kids and my brother's kids experienced the joy and purity of a grandparent's love. All our kids were very close to them. Especially my daughter Marlene. She loved my mother the most, and was the closest to her.

As a father, I feel and I understand so many things now that I didn't before. All my life, I'd heard people tell me that certain things'll only make sense to me when I become a dad myself. Which I didn't really believe back then, but I do now. Seeing my children grow up to become amazing human beings fills my heart with joy like no other success or accomplishment could.

After my father died, we saw my mother go through the worst time ever. She tried her best to fight everything and cope, but somehow, no matter how hard she tried, nothing could make the pain of losing her husband go away.

We saw her stay strong and fight whatever came in her way, and we saw her give up and breakdown when she missed my dad a bit much and couldn't take it. Even though my brother went to stay with her for some time, nothing could compare to what my dad meant to her.

She started keeping herself busy – trying anything and everything to distract herself enough to not miss him. But all her efforts went in vain. After a while, my mother was diagnosed with depression, and unfortunately, it kept getting worse. After a long, hard battle, she finally gave up once and for all, and she passed away in the summer of 2017 when I was on a fishing trip away from home.

When I think about my parents now, I try to not feel sad. I try to take each day as it comes, and I've decided to always dedicate my life to practising everything they taught me – everything that they valued and all that was important to them. They were great people, and I feel fortunate and blessed to have had a relationship with them as I did.

I try to teach my kids almost the same things that my parents teach me. The same values, the same lifestyle, and the same traditions. I just want the best for my kids. I want them to be happy in their own lives, I want them to succeed in their careers, in their marriages, and in everything that they do.

I sometimes can't help but feel that I didn't get to live the fairytale love that I saw my parents live. There are days when I can't help but think why it didn't work out with any three of my wives. I know that they had nothing against me because, like I said, we co-parent, and we're on friendly terms, even today. Which says a lot about a person even after you've separated from them.

I've always felt like regrets are the stupidest thing to ever exist. Remorse, guilt, grief – those are all feelings I value and respect. But to me, regret means nothing. In my life, after experiencing several unpleasant experiences, I came to a conclusion; regret is absolutely useless.

Yes, you get to learn a lesson. But that's what you call experience. Regretting something is whining about what you can't change in the past. We're all aware that under no circumstances can the past ever be changed. So, trying to change something you can't. Or wishing to turn back time is absolutely useless.

You take each day as it comes, and you learn to live with it. There are two sides to everything – this applies to every experience you go through in life. You take something good from it, and you move on.

There is no way of knowing for sure what you can expect from someone in life. No way but to experience it yourself. And once you've experienced that very thing, it can't be undone. If it can't be undone, there is no point of regret. Regret is just a way of justifying causing mental unease and distress to oneself.

Anyways. After thinking about all the things in the world – good and bad, it was finally time for me to board. I couldn't believe it; the moment was finally here. I was ecstatic, and I couldn't wait to see my family.

I also couldn't wait to get home and personally thank everyone who helped me. I feel immensely blessed, and I believe that the situation could've been so much worse if I didn't have a few people helping me.

Mainly my brother Wesley. Who, even from a whole other country, proved to be one of the greatest resources ever! The way he had me facilitated and took care of all the paperwork and funds – I was amazed and grateful, not the least bit surprised. Because that's just the kind of kind person he is.

My daughters went through a lot of stress and trouble too. The captain told me that they were constantly in touch with the captain enquiring about me. They kept asking about my physical health, what shape I was in, my mental health (due to the trauma of losing Carl and Motorboat), and everything else. Even things that I didn't care to think of.

Sometimes, it takes an occurrence as unfortunate as the one I endured, but, in the end, it makes you realize the bigger picture. After weathering the storm, my sun was finally shining. And it was shining brighter than ever!

Hurricane IRMA

When the storm hit, I couldn't believe what was going on. It's like my body and my mind took several minutes to process all that was going on around me. It was all a very overwhelming experience, but now that I look back on it, it made me realize the amount of stress I have.

God, it also opened my eyes to the power of having faith. I think I can safely say that my faith is what got me through most of my time while I was stranded on the boat, in the middle of the sea – as one of the worst storms broke. I was scared to death; I'm not going to lie. But it got me thinking a lot. For instance, what exactly is the purpose of life?

I know we all came into this world for a reason, but how do you know when you've accomplished all that you were sent to? I've been thinking about it a lot recently, and I can't exactly come up with any right answer.

Maybe there is no right answer. Maybe we're all just living through life, trying to do the best we can to make our mark and leave this world better than it was. People say that bad things happen for a reason. Some others believe that the reason people believe that is because they're trying to glorify their misfortune.

I, for one, believe the latter to be completely incorrect. I believe that bad things happen for a reason, and I also believe that it doesn't necessarily have to mean that we're trying to find an excuse to cover something terrible that happened to us.

I genuinely believe that God puts us in these positions because He wants us to take something from them and make significant changes in our lives, even if it's something as seemingly trivial as paying attention to the little things in life, which is why, ever since the accident, I've taken it upon myself to thank God for all His blessings in life regularly and to be grateful always.

It's been over two years since Hurricane IRMA, but I still remember every single moment like it was just yesterday.

My heart starts racing every time I think about the moment when we realized the storm had broken. There was panic, commotion, and just understandable fear everywhere, as we rushed back and forth on the boat, trying to figure out what to do next.

Moments before the hurricane closed in, I was in the freezer with my tools, trying to get it up and running again. I didn't know what was going on since the freezer is located at the boat's bottom.

Carl and I knew there was a storm coming in, and we thought we were prepared. But then again, we couldn't have, in our wildest imagination, ever thought the storm would turn out to be one of the worst hurricanes the country has ever witnessed.

And just like that, in the blink of an eye, the boat started to sink. Carl and I both start to freak out because none of us could figure out what to do. Before we knew it, the water had started to make its well into the boat. I tried to get the life raft to inflate immediately so that Carl and I could get in it. I tied it to the front handrail at the back of the cabin.

At that moment, we were dead in the water. We were in contact with the coast guard every thirty minutes or so, as he tried to talk us through the plan and navigate us to safety. The coast guard told us about Carnival, the ship that had made its way somewhere close by as it ran from the storm, just like we were trying to.

Except, Carnival wasn't from Florida; it had come from the Bahamas. I tried to establish contact with the captain there, and I managed to do so around 5 pm successfully, which was around three whole hours of us, desperately calling out for help.

The water had begun to make it challenging to get around the boat, but I still chose not to panic too much. Because this was my first time on a sinking boat, Carl had been on sinking boats before. Which is why I let him take the lead on this one. I was waiting for Carl to tell me when to get off the boat.

The captain informed us that Carnival was still about 3 hours away. Carl was pacing the boat with his life jacket on as I monitored the radio to respond from the coast guard and the captain. The boat had nearly sunken, and now, I was beginning to get worried. The raft was still where I had tied it, just in case. And the captain was on his way to get us. I was checking with him every thirty minutes.

I had Motorboat with me in a carrier, I was all set to abandon my boat and get into the water, but I couldn't find Carl anywhere, which is when I started to worry. After 2 hours at around 7:30, I heard Carl call out to me and tell me that we need to get off the boat as soon as possible.

The water was rushing in from all sides, and there was barely any space left on the boat for us to hang on to. I cut the rope off the raft, and I yelled for Carl to get into the raft. The captain at Carnival was around 7 miles away, and it was starting to get dark. Fortunately, we had flashlights, and our life jackets each had mirrors and whistles to help locate us.

Earlier, when I had spoken to Carl, we brainstormed through rescue strategies. I had told Carl that it might come to that, judging by the current situation. Carl packed a bag off of his belongings on the boat. I even remember telling him not to do so. Carnival was being sent to rescue us; I wasn't sure they'd be too thrilled to know we had a bag of personal belongings accompanying us.

Carl and I talked about getting on the raft. He was hesitant for some reason, and I didn't exactly know why. I told him that when they'd come to rescue us, there is a possibility that they might not lower the lifeboats as the captain told us. This was due to the extra rough weather conditions.

The water continued rising. We were now struggling to find a spot to stand and figure out what to do because our boat was sinking. The coast guard asked us to abandon the boat and get on the life raft – but Carl didn't like the idea. The waters were *very* unsteady, and we didn't know what else to do. At that moment, I didn't think I had the time to convince Carl or question why he chose not to do as the captain said. So, I tried to take the lead, hoping Carl would follow.

I grabbed Motorboat and began to cut the ropes of the raft free. I couldn't let Motorboat go. And I couldn't find Carl either. I knew he was somewhere on the boat, but I couldn't see him.

I knew Carl didn't want to get on the raft, but I needed to find him and get him on the raft. When the coast guard asked us if we could swim, Carl didn't answer, which was weird because I feel like I maybe should've known whether or not Carl knew how to swim.

So, I didn't know whether or not Carl could swim. I needed to think and act fast, so I took my pocket knife out. I was in an absolute panic mode, and I didn't know if we were going to make it even though the worst hadn't happened yet.

I somehow managed to spot the cruise ship on the horizon, and I breathed a tiny sigh of relief. I cut the first two ropes of the boat and struggled to stay on board. The waters were extreme, and I was carrying Motorboat in a carrier.

All of a sudden, the boat moved way too rapidly and made a big jump. This caused the raft to hit me in the face, and it knocked Motorboat right out of my hand.

I broke my glasses, and I dropped Motorboat. Right in front of my eyes, I lost him. And the worst part is that I didn't even have a single second to process it because every second was precious. The boat was going down very fast, and I needed to find Carl and get him into the raft. But it was dark by then, and I couldn't find Carl anywhere. I was beginning to worry about him now.

We both had our life jackets on, and I was in a rut. I didn't know which way to go. I couldn't see Carl, and I had just lost Motorboat. I couldn't process whatever was happening because there was way too much chaos, and I didn't do well under pressure. Everything was happening way too fast for me even to be able to accept it. I didn't know where to go, and the radio was on the boat, which had sunk right before my eyes.

I was torn between saving my own life and getting on the raft or getting Carl on it before I go, but at the same time, I'd be risking my life because the boat had already sunk – right in front of my eyes.

I took a leap of faith and got on the raft. I cut all the ends of it free and got into the water on the raft. I figured I'd just look for Carl from the raft because the boat had already sunk. So, if he had to be somewhere, it'd be in the water, and I knew for a fact that I'd be able to help him way more from the raft than I would've from the boat.

I kept looking at the lights on the ship, but I didn't know how I'd get there. The water was very rough, and I didn't even know if the captain on the ship could have the lifeboats lowered down because the water and the winds were so rough, as suspected. I was worried about Carl, and I didn't want anything to happen to him.

I had no idea how I was going to reach the captain. I didn't even know how I would get to him because the waters were very rough – nothing like I had ever seen before. It stressed me out just looking at those giant waves crashing into one another. All I could imagine was being tossed from one wave to another.

I got onto the raft, and there was still no sign of Carl. There was no sign of Carnival either. I was starting to get stressed now. I yelled as I always hoped for him to hear me somehow. No luck.

I was waiting in the raft, and the boat was now minutes away from completely sinking. Which is precisely when I heard Carl call out my name:

"Eddie! Eddie! Eddie!" he said.

I looked at him, and I tried my best to somehow get to him, but I couldn't. Because he had already almost gone down with the boat, and I couldn't get the raft to him in time.

So, there was nothing I could do except watch him go down with the boat. And every time I mention this awful sentence, a part of me just breaks, and I can't stop thinking about it. Part of me can't help but feel guilty for not being able to save Carl.

Even though there was nothing I could've done to save him. And I know that if there was anything, *anything* I could've done – I would've done it. I didn't get to save either of them; Motorboat or Carl, which haunts me, even to this day.

I sat in the raft, waiting for Carnival to come to rescue me. At that moment, even though I tried my best to keep the faith, even the fact that I was going to be rescued seemed like a long-shot to me, unfortunately. I waited, sitting in the raft for about half an hour, in the middle of the storm until I finally saw some light approaching.

I cannot explain how I felt at that moment. It's as if my life had turned around in a single second. My heart was bursting with joy, and all my prayers had been answered. As I saw the lights on the Carnival approach, my heart beat faster the closer they got. It was a Godsent miracle. It's like it was a light in the dark, exactly how my life felt at that moment.

Which really got me thinking about so much stuff. Mainly, why did I get to survive this? Could there be a special reason? How could I have possibly made it through everything that happened? It all seemed unreal, and I was very overwhelmed.

I started flailing my arms like crazy, and I blew on my whistle, hoping they'd hear me. I started swinging my flashlight as I signaled SOS. And, it worked. The captain had spotted me. That was another huge sigh of relief. I can't imagine what I'd have gone through if nobody had spotted me. I would've died in that water.

The hard part was over. Now, all that was left to do was to get onto the ship and regain my energy and strength. Because believe it or not, but planning and executing your own rescue really takes the life out of you.

When the captain lowered the ladder for me to jump on to, I couldn't reach it. Even though I had a rope around my arms and my chest, between the high tides and moving ship, I just couldn't. I remember feeling so weak and almost giving up. I didn't know what to do. But then I remembered all the phone calls with my daughters just hours ago. I couldn't get their pleading voices out of my head.

I heard my daughters begging me to fight and to be okay. Which meant I had absolutely no choice but to give my daughters precisely what they asked for. So, I used up every ounce of strength I had to reach the ladder and climb onto the boat. And I finally made it on board.

Once I got on the boat, I fell down on the ground, and everyone thought I'd collapsed because of all the trauma my body had endured to get here. The captain, first officers, and the entire medical team gathered to help me.

They got me onto a wheelchair and took me to the infirmary. I couldn't believe how nice the people were. It was *JUST* what I needed at that moment, after surviving the absolute worst. The captain came up to me and made sure I was okay, and he made sure I'd get all the help I needed. The captain was a saint. Everyone from Carnival that was helping me was a saint.

They were the most helpful people I had ever met. They rushed me to the infirmary, did a full workup, and got me checked for everything possible. After three hours, they moved me to a cabin because I needed rest.

When they moved me to the cabin, they gave me dry clothes to change into, shoes, and food. I didn't even realize how long it had been since I hadn't eaten. That bowl of soup seemed like heaven to me. Especially because of the level of hospitality it came with.

The captain's name was Gigliotti. He was such a fine gentleman. One of the best I've ever met in a long, long time. I know for a fact that if it wasn't for him, I wouldn't have made it through that terrifying ordeal, the way I did. I want to thank him every day for his compassion and hospitality.

I stayed in that cabin for about two more days as we made our way to Freeport, Bahamas. The captain and his team took me to the top deck to call someone in my family from my satellite phone. Unfortunately, the only phone number I had memorized was my wife's number. So, I had no choice but to call her, which was not what I wanted to do at all, considering that we had technically separated.

Stranded

Even though I'm on my way home now, I still couldn't believe that I somehow managed to survive all that had happened to me the past week. I thought the storm was going to be the worst thing I'd have to endure in all of this terrifying ordeal, but I was wrong.

The hard part was over, but that didn't mean I'd have no more challenges to face. I felt awful because I believed I was putting so many people through so much trouble to help me get out there. On the bright side, I felt lucky to have had people who went out of their way to ensure my safe return – but it wasn't easy.

On my way to Freeport from where the captain rescued me, it was a terrible situation. I was lucky to be alive, and I had somehow made it through without any injuries. God's plan, I guess. Anyone who saw the storm would not believe that could've been possible. It was an awful hurricane, and anyone who had enough courage to make it into the water wouldn't have any way of knowing whether or not he'd be able to make it out alive.

So, the entire journey on the Carnival was a bit of a relief for me, but it was hell for my family, unfortunately. Since there was no way of communicating from the ship to Florida, all my family could know was that I was safe. No more, no less.

I remember my daughters were freaking out, and the wait was killing them. All everyone wanted to know was if I was okay, after knowing that I was safe and that I had been rescued. I didn't know this at the time, but my daughter was in constant contact with the communication officer. She was desperately trying to figure out what state I was in. She even went on to ask the captain if I had any broken bones or internal bleeding.

Unfortunately, all they could be told was that a man was rescued. Nothing beyond that for a while. My nephew emailed the captain and asked them if the one man they had rescued was a tall white male, to which the captain replied, "yes." This was a relief for my family. Carl was a black male with an average height and build.

Once my family got the satisfaction of knowing that I was alive, things got better for a day, and I had hoped they'd be able to sleep peacefully throughout the night without worrying about me. What's surprising is that almost everything seemed to work out before I got off the boat in freeport.

I was told I couldn't get off without any documentation, and my brother Wesley was informed about that by the captain. So, he made arrangements for me by the time I got to the Bahamas. I still won't ever forget the terrifying journey from the rescue to the moment I got off the ship, safe and sound. It all seemed like a dream – too good to be true.

If I had to guess how I made it, I would give all the credit to the prayers of my family. I was there, so I know just how unlikely it was for someone to survive whatever I survived. Which is why I want to thank them every single day. Not just because they prayed for my safe return and rescue, but for strengthening my faith in God.

I always had faith in God and his miracles. But this divine intervention caused my belief to grow even stronger than it did in all these years.

There was a series of events that convinced me that the only reason I made it out alive was because of God and his help. In a chaotic situation like the event before the rescue, when I hadn't left the boat yet, I put on my survival suit while talking to my son. He knew about the storm, and by the looks of it, he guessed it'd be pretty worse in the next few hours.

I had already told him about the situation at that time, and I even ran by him the possibility of abandoning the boat because back then, the water had already started to come into it. My mind wasn't working at all in all that panic and chaos.

So, my son Eddie who helped me realize while talking to me that I didn't need the survival suit if I was going to get off the boat, all I needed was a lifejacket. A survival suit is bulky, and it has gloves attached, which would've made it very hard for me to grab on to the ladder of the ship during the rescue.

I consider something which seemed so insignificant (back then) to be a blessing – now that I look back on it. These were all signs of God's help, which I now realize.

The first angel, however, was Carl. He was the one who told me we needed to go. If it wasn't for him, we never would've known, and I wouldn't be alive today. I miss Carl, and I really do hope that he is looking down on me from heaven. He practically saved me, and for that, all the words in the world couldn't express my gratitude.

On the day after the rescue (my second day on the Carnival), the first officer came to see me after the medical officer had taken my blood pressure. The first officer asked me to write a statement on everything that had happened and to describe the events. I told him that I could write whatever part of it I remembered, but I didn't have my glasses, since I lost them during the rescue.

They told me that it was okay and asked me to get some rest. The next day, they came to visit me again and brought a pair of reader glasses, which surprisingly helped me. I wrote a three-page statement and asked to keep the reader glasses. Again, one of the many things which were very unlikely to happen and eventually turned out to be a great help, the reader glasses they gave.

Those glasses turned out to be a lifesaver during all the paperwork we went through in Nassau and Freeport.

This is another thing I thank God for. What were the chances of me finding reader glasses after a rescue? It was all God's blessings. And he continued to bless me with one thing after the other.

Here's the statement I wrote on the ship before we got to Freeport:

"We left out shrimping around August 27th, 2017. Things were good until Irma came by. Watching the weather channel, we thought it would go up the east coast of Florida. Instead, it went up the west coast. Very big and high winds. We were by Ft. Jefferson. I got worried and ran about 50 miles Southwest to avoid Irma. When the storm started Northwest, I turned back to Ft. Jefferson. The boat started taking on water. I started cleaning the pump strainers. I went into the freezer to tighten the stuffing box and got it slowed down. My tool bucket had turned over in the bilge. With all the rocking, I could not find the tools, so I went back to the engine room to go clean the strainer. I'm 61 years old, and I had been throwing up all day. Carl Shephard was 71 and was to stay on deck only. I got overwhelmed and wore slam out – I couldn't continue. I couldn't get the coast guard on the radio, so I called my wife to tell her we needed help, but I had no access to the area, and we had no fuel. So, we continued to call for pumps. No luck. The 3-71 stopped first, and a couple of hours later, the main engine stopped. We dropped anchor and continued talking to the coastguard every 30 minutes. I got the raft down the starboard side. Carl had been on sinking boats before, so he asked to stay on the big boat. I had never been on a sinking boat before, so I asked him to let me know when it was time to get in the raft. Carl told me we had plenty of time, so we got in touch with the coastguard, and he informed us the estimated time of arrival for Carnival was around 3 hours. We had two lines on the raft. Just before it got dark, Carl hollers 'Eddie, we gotta go, we gotta go.' He asked me to go out of the starboard wheelhouse door. Water began to rush very quickly. I ran out of the door with my cat. The raft lunged up, knocking me back under the eaves. I panicked, dropped the cat, and jumped in the water, and swam to the raft. I cut the front tie-up line. I saw Carl still on the boat. I said, 'Carl get in the water,' but at that second, the boat went straight down at a 45°. The other line tied to the boat spun me around and started pulling me down but snapped. I lost all views of Carl. All I saw mast and boom go under the sea, so fast. I hollered for Carl for a while. The speed the boat went down in was unbelievable. Then Carnival showed up about an hour later."

After I got to Freeport, there was a lot of back and forth for the documents, the reservations, and the bookings, and other legalities and technicalities. One of the moments I remember very well is when I first spoke to my oldest daughter Marlene; when I got to the embassy, Ms. Wallace already had Marlene on the phone for me.

I remember crying like a little baby. I couldn't believe all that I had managed to survive, and something about hearing my daughter's voice gave me so much hope and strength that I allowed myself to breakdown after everything I had been through. It was a moment I'll remember forever. Every step of the way, remembering my kids has given me immense strength to carry on.

If someone had asked me if I would've been able to get through something this major and difficult, I would've said 'no' in a heartbeat because I obviously never thought I had it in me. When I looked back at that night almost three years ago, all I can remember is the fight in me, fueled by the love I have for my children and the love I have for God.

And I thank God every day for that. If it was any of my kids who got stuck in such a terrible situation, I wouldn't have made it through. Not knowing where and how my kids are would've killed me. This gives me all the more reason to realize just how blessed I truly am to have my kids. The strength they possess is beyond extraordinary.

So basically, after three long, hard days, and after going back and forth all the time, I was finally set to be on my way back home. It was *NOT* easy at all.

Between not having room to stay in, not having anything to my name, the trouble with all official documentation, trouble speaking to my family back home, not having a picture for my emergency passport (and later on, not having clothes I could be photographed in for the photo), to basically every other hiccup that I endured on my journey back home, the one thing I made sure I never did was to give up.

By the time I got on board at the carnival, I had already realized how gracious God had been. He saved me and helped me find a way to get home safely. Which is why I made it a point to always be grateful and count my blessings.

I figured, if I was lucky enough to weather the storm and survive, I have a purpose in life. Even after all these years and having lived the life I did.

After everything that had happened, I realized one thing: I made my way to the boarding hall. I realized that this was going to stay with me forever. I knew that I'd have to tell this story a million times again.

And I knew that every time I told the story, I'd have to relive the worst moments of my life. For instance, now, even though I'm on my way home and everything seems fine, the fact that the TSA guy asked me about my emergency passport just a few minutes ago has already given me a glimpse into what life is going to be like. I don't know if I'm prepared for it or not, but I know that either way, it's going to be one hell of a challenge.

For that moment, I only tried focusing on the positives. Like the fact that I was hours away from hugging my children and my brothers. And that I was going to get to sleep in my own bed tonight, under my own roof and that I'd be back in my country – where I didn't expect to have any problem at all.

I knew my family couldn't wait to see me, and that more importantly, I couldn't wait to see them. All I looked forward to was to get home as soon as possible so that I could be at peace, and all this could finally be over.

Finally, I boarded the plane and waited for the longest 90 minutes of my life to pass by. I don't know how I managed to make it through the entire flight without falling apart. I was anxious, and I was trembling.

I tried getting some rest on the flight home. I even tried to sleep for a little bit, but I couldn't. I don't know if it was anxious to get home or to be able to breathe a sigh of relief once we finally land. Because at that moment, after all that had happened, everything seemed too good to be true.

The captain made the landing announcement, and as soon as he did, my heart started beating faster and faster. I honestly didn't even know how I made it through all those stops and checks because I remember wanting to rush past it all and just hug my daughters.

I was also hoping somehow my soon to be ex-wife would have the courtesy to be respectful and not show up. Considering her and I were separated, I didn't think she had any business being there with me at an intimate moment like that. But all I could do was hope.

When I got off the plane, I felt completely lost. I don't know if it was the fact that I couldn't process all the emotions or if I was just experiencing post-traumatic stress disorder (PTSD). I knew everything, I knew what to do, but I somehow still went the wrong way and forgot about the tram.

I was walking very slow, and I just seemed off and low. But when I got to the terminal and looked through the glass and saw my daughters and my brothers, my heart was bursting with joy. I rushed past everyone as fast as I could, and I walked towards the gate. I couldn't believe it; they were all standing right there!

There are no words to describe what I was feeling at that moment. It was a very emotional moment for everyone. My family is everything to me. They are the foundation of everything that I am. Without them, I wouldn't have made it through any of this. Their love and constant support are what got me through it all, and for that, there aren't enough words in the world to thank God.

"Captain, can you tell me where my dad is?"

As I made my way towards the gate to greet my family, it was such an overwhelming moment for me, and for them too, I'm sure. Everything felt like a dream come true. I saw my wife standing there too. My brother and children were there too, and so was my good friend, Rick.

I know we weren't exactly a happy couple, and people could tell. But something about still being associated with my wife bothered me. To make things worse, I didn't know, but the press was there too.

Coincidently, my wife and I had the exact same colored shirts on – which screamed happy couple, but in reality, it was anything but. I didn't even know where we stood. I mean, I knew. But I wasn't entirely sure that she did.

I felt a bit out of place, and I definitely felt uncomfortable. I was supposed to be focused on my family, the people who mean the world to me. Instead, all I felt was confused. I was confused about what was going on with her. And had she completely forgotten that we were getting a divorce?

I walked towards them and hugged my daughter first. It was honestly the best feeling in the world. I was already expecting to get a bit emotional, but I wasn't exactly prepared to be crying.

I stepped out of Gate "A" and immediately hugged my daughter. I cannot find the right words to describe how great it felt to be seeing those faces after I thought I'd never get to see them again.

I felt like the luckiest man in the world. But at the same time, I couldn't help but think how terrible it must have been for Carl's family. They didn't get to see him come back. I felt gutted to just think about the fact that they were never going to see him again.

This was an amazing moment for me. Unfortunately, my ex-wife's crocodile tears were starting to get to me. Seeing all the people I love standing there waiting for me was probably the best sight I've ever witnessed. I can surely say that not even the rescue made me feel as alive as hugging my loved ones did.

Even though I was thinking about Carl a lot, I didn't want to talk about him. I was still pretty shaken by all the trauma that led to losing him. A lot was going on in my mind at the time. My ex-wife's questionable behavior, the overwhelming joy of getting to hug my daughters again, my brothers were telling me how relieved they were and, most of all, the grieving of Carl that I never really got around to.

When I spoke to my brother Wesley afterward, he told me that he'd gotten to the airport a bit earlier, and my wife was there too. When he saw all the press waiting for my arrival, he asked her, "what's with all the press?" and she said, "well, Edwards got a story to tell."

I can't exactly comment on what her intentions were by doing so, but it's not something I needed at that moment. I was already very traumatized, and I didn't get the chance to process all that had happened fully. Even though I appreciated the support and people coming out to commend me for my efforts, I didn't need the press to be there.

There were many legalities and technicalities that I knew I'd have to deal with a while later, and I feel that the press only made it worse in terms of my mental state and pressure. When my wife approached me at the airport, she put her arms around me and hugged me. I wish I could say it's what I wanted, but I didn't. I didn't know how to react.

I froze for a second. I was lost and confused. I thought to myself, 'do I hug her; do I kiss her? Who is this woman?' and I just let it be. I do remember that it was a terrible feeling. I was married to this woman, and I committed and intended to spend the rest of my life with her. But all she was to me at that moment, was a stranger.

It's funny because you think you know someone, which is precisely why you plan on spending the rest of your lives with them, but it doesn't work out. I've gone through this before, which is exactly why I didn't understand why I was surprised. I guess I expected the third time to be the charm. But I was wrong.

Again, I was trying to focus on the positive and just be there for my kids, but I hate the fact that I let it bother me so much. Especially in a time when I know just how much my kids needed me. Whenever I think about the mental state they were in while I was stuck at sea, I feel super proud of having raised such strong kids.

I keep reading the emails Marlene and the captain exchanged while I wasn't in touch with them during the hurricane. I feel like tears run down my face every time I read them. My daughter went as far as asking the captain whether Motorboat was alive *just* so she knew what state I was in. I don't know what I did to deserve so much love. But I thank God all the time.

I read one where she says, "Captain, can you tell me where my dad is?" and I got chills. I remember how close I was to my father, and I also remember the toll his death took on me. Whenever I think about my daughter, worried out of her mind, not knowing where her father is, I break-a little inside.

I don't know how I'd be able to sleep at night if I didn't know where my father was. Especially if he was in the middle of the sea during one of the worst hurricanes in the country, I applaud her bravery; God bless her heart. I can't believe the level of compassion she possesses. It surprises me more and more each day.

Even though she knew I'd made it safely on to the boat and that I'd be on my home soon, she still asked the captain every single small detail just to ensure that she does her best to take care of me and be there for me in every aspect possible.

Watching her grow up to be one of the most remarkable women I've ever seen fills my heart with joy. And even though she's got a family of her own now, she'll always be my little girl.

I love that kid to death; she's everything to me. And it's safe to say that I wouldn't have made it through so much in life if it wasn't for all my children's love and support.

So, at the airport, I noticed my wife's attitude change. And not in a good way, I'm afraid. I thought she hugged me in the heat of the moment at the airport or because it was an emotional time for everyone involved. But it turns out; she was behaving like everything was A-Okay between us.

To be honest, it scared me a bit because I didn't know what to make of it. Before I had left, she was cold as ice to me. And now she was being super considerate and trying to act we were still a married couple.

Which, technically, we were. But no way wouldn't change soon. Because we'd already decided on a divorce, and she'd already told me about her new boyfriend.

I couldn't just assume she'd decided to leave him and come back to me after she got the scare of losing me to the hurricane. And even if she did, it doesn't work like that. Because, in my opinion, there is no place for adultery in a marriage. No matter how miserable or bored you are, it's just simply unacceptable.

I was finally starting to realize that I didn't want her in my life; neither did I need her. Because of what she had done to me and our marriage, I had a hard time believing that there'd ever been a way for us to recover from this. She could've fixed things.

Instead, she chose to have an affair and end our marriage for good. And that isn't the kind of person I want to be with, ever.

So, I got back home, and luckily, my brother decided to stay for a few more days. I put the marriage drama aside for a while and decided to deal with it later. I had a lot to take care of – insurance company troubles, dealing with lawyers, and so much more. I just couldn't bear the thought of dealing with everything *and* her all at once.

The insurance company supplied me with an attorney for Carl's family to receive money as a settlement of some sort. They took money out of my insurance account for my boat and my home owner's account.

At the same time, I was dealing with a divorce lawyer because I had asked one to get the paperwork ready to send to my ex-wife so we could get it done with and out of the way.

My ex-wife stayed for a couple of days after I got back but went back to her house after telling her I'd be proceeding with the divorce. Her house was partly damaged because of the hurricane, so I offered to stay longer if she liked, but she chose not to.

After the divorce, I suffered from PTSD. Not because of the divorce. But because it all happened at once and I couldn't get my thoughts together. I had difficulty getting regular things done, and I felt like I just wasn't in the right headspace.

The support of my family made everything alright, though. I couldn't imagine what I would've done if it wasn't for them. After a year, I finally decided to go for therapy. This was back when everything got too much for me to handle, unfortunately.

I'm really grateful for everything my family has done for me. Their compassion and patience with me have been remarkable, to say the least. There was a time when I started to feel like I maybe needed companionship. But whenever I thought about it, it just ended up giving me major anxiety.

There were days when I missed being married and having someone to come home to, but nothing compared to the after-effects of the divorce. I didn't think I had it in me to go through all that again. If it weren't for therapy or the support of my family, I wouldn't have made it through any of it. But I'm glad I opted for therapy.

Therapy helped me get back to my routine. It helped me to slowly start taking control of my own life again – which, unfortunately, I'd lost with time due to the PTSD from the hurricane and my divorce.

Before I started therapy, I was in somewhat of a dark place. I was depressed. I had just retired, so I wasn't going shrimping, which meant I had a lot of time on my hands. And that didn't work out too well, unfortunately. I was 61 years old when I retired. Retirement and that age paired with depression was just a recipe for disaster.

People tend not to talk about depression. I always knew it was an awful thing. I just didn't know how bad it was until I experienced it myself. Nothing felt right. Even though I had my family's support and love, I still felt like something was missing.

I'd always believed in God's countless blessings. And even though God didn't withhold any of his blessings, I still felt like something wasn't right. I was beginning to lose my appetite, I felt low and dizzy, and I never had enough energy.

It got so worse; I found myself experiencing great difficulty doing the things that I usually loved to do. I didn't even want to see anyone. I just distanced myself from everyone and everything.

When my family started to notice that this was something much more serious than it initially was, they decided to get me the help that I needed. And I'm so glad they did.

After I did therapy regularly, I started to feel a lot better. I was six months away from all the insurance technicalities finally getting cleared. So, I thought of buying another boat. I loved the idea of being out there again.

I'd always loved the sea. I was a third-generation shrimper, and for as long as I can remember, I've loved the sea. Most of my childhood was spent on a boat because my parents always made sure we had one.

I spent the later years of my life also on a boat. I managed to make my entire living doing what I loved – being out at sea.

But lately, the thought of buying another boat didn't sit right. Even though it excited me at first, later I figured that it'd be too much of a hassle for me. With the maintenance and everything, I just didn't want to be doing all that again.

Being at my age, dealing with crew members, and the possibility of ending up in another storm didn't feel like the best idea at all. And even if I was shrimping, I knew I didn't want to do it enough to make a living out of it anymore.

The fuel is highly-priced, the shrimps aren't enough to cover all the costs – it just didn't seem worth it to me anymore.

So that's how I finally decided to retire. I started getting my social security and decided to spend some time doing things that I loved. Things I wanted to do, not things that I needed to do. I started traveling a bit. It's not like I took off on a world tour within a week, but I did things that were fun.

I started visiting my family more often. If I needed to take a road trip, to see my family or friends, it just meant that I didn't have to think twice because I had no commitments. I could just take off and stay for as long as I liked. And that felt amazing.

It sure feels different, but I'm enjoying every bit of it. I got two cats, which have helped me feel a lot better about everything around me. After losing Motorboat, it took me a while to realize that I wanted another animal.

What some people don't realize is how terrible it is to lose a pet. I'm a cat guy, and I had always considered Motorboat as family.

I was very attached to her, and after I lost her in the hurricane, everything just seemed off whenever I thought about getting another pet.

I love cats, but part of me just couldn't process losing Motorboat. Especially because of the way it all happened. When Motorboat died, I was in the middle of battling death myself. I tried to save my own life, and I watched Carl and Motorboat die right in front of me.

I know there's nothing I could've done to save Motorboat, but whenever I think about what I could've done, I end up feeling gutted. There's this inevitable guilt that just eats me up, and I hate it.

That was part of the reason that I found it so difficult to get another pet. Because I hadn't fully recovered from the loss of Motorboat, I know it sounds like a funny thing for a guy my age to be saying, but I loved Motorboat.

For the longest time, it was just us. At home and on the boat, so obviously, I was very attached to her.

In my opinion, animals are just like human beings in terms of feelings and emotions. Pets tend to develop a very strong liking towards their owners. This is primarily why they have such protective instincts. They constantly need your undivided attention, love, and care. And Motorboat was my absolute favorite.

Even though I truly miss Motorboat a lot, I'm glad I decided to get another pet. I ended up getting two cats after Motorboat, and it's been so much better ever since they've been around. It's surely been way less lonely. And it feels good to have someone around. Better a cat than another wife, I'll say.

The day I landed in Tampa back from the Bahamas, I remember seeing security officers all around the area where my family waited for my arrival. Even though I didn't know this back then, it wasn't because of me. It wasn't because of any special protection or any protocol, either. But it's because my daughter and ex-wife had an agreement when the press got there.

My daughters tried to make the experience as easy for me as possible. They knew I didn't want any press around at that moment. But my wife had invited them without checking with any of my family members before.

My daughters knew what I was going through, and they also knew exactly what I needed at that moment – it was anything but the press.

One of the reasons my daughters didn't want the press there was because they were worried I'd say something to incriminate myself, and that may be a lawyer could later use that against me.

That's just the level of concern my daughters have for me – unlike my ex-wife, unfortunately. That's just one of the many reasons why I love my girls so much. They've gone out of their way and done everything in their power to be there for me. And to make everything better, to help in any way they can.

I'll never be able to thank them enough or tell them what they mean to me. Whenever I think about their efforts and what they went through when I was stuck in the middle of a hurricane, I feel blessed. And I thank God for blessing me with the sweetest girls anyone could've ever imagined.

Bankruptcy and hopelessness

Lately, life had been tough for me, to say the least. It was like I couldn't catch a break. Even though the storm had passed and I had managed to survive it, nothing changed for me. No matter how hard I tried, I kept getting caught up in one mess after the other.

My wife wanted to patch things up with me, but I was sure that ship had sailed. I didn't want her anymore. When she told me about her affair, it's like someone reached into my chest and yanked my heart out. It felt awful, and part of my depression came from my third divorce. It was just the idea of not being able to stay married to someone I love for as long as I'd like to.

I started letting guilt consume me, and everything went downhill from there. I couldn't eat, couldn't function properly, and I couldn't think straight at all. I felt hopeless and miserable. It was all too much, even for a 62-year-old man, actually, especially for a 62-year-old man. I needed a break. And to top it all off, I didn't even have a boat. Neither did I want one, ever again.

My boat meant a lot to me. It was an escape for me. And right now, I feel like I really needed that escape. Things weren't looking good for me – in any aspect. My love life had failed, once again. My mental health was in shambles, I lost the only friend I had to sail with, and I had become the cause of my family's worries.

I never imagined I'd be in a place like this. All I wanted to do was cry, but I didn't let myself do even that. Something about being a man has this preset notion about being all tough and stable in every way. I was in a very dark place, and I felt like being given a chance to break down would actually help me.

I was getting the help I needed, but at times, I still felt helpless. I felt hopeless. I began to find things to blame my hopelessness on. It was a very unconventional coping mechanism, yes. But I was hoping it'd help. I convinced myself that the void in my life was due to the lack of companionship. But that didn't last long.

I remembered how miserable I was with my third wife, Joanna. And everything came back. I then convinced myself that I wasn't feeling the way I did due to the lack of companionship, but it was because I was just overwhelmed. I couldn't help myself, and I couldn't help my family. All I could see them try to do was help me, but I made it very difficult for them. And that made me feel worse.

I was having a hard time coping. I missed being on the boat; I missed the water and shrimping. Life changed way too fast for me, and I was doing a terrible job at accustoming to the changes. I was used to being around my wife, I was used to being able to call my mom or go see her, I was used to being on the boat and shrimping – then celebrating my wining catches with Carl, and I couldn't do any of that.

It was all taking a toll on me. But even despite all that, I found reasons to feel blessed. I convinced myself that I was stronger than this. And I believed that God could move mountains. I thought about how I got saved from the storm. That night, to say that there was no hope for me to survive would be an understatement.

There was no living being in-sight; I was floating in the dark waters, all by myself. In the middle of all the debris that surrounded me. I was in the middle of a storm, and honestly, I was prepared to die. I wasn't ready, but I had prepared myself by making peace with the fact that literally, anything could happen.

I didn't know what else to do. I was a wreck. I remember feeling the most scared and terrified I've ever felt in my life. It's like I stared death in the eye and somehow made it back alive. Everything about that night still sends chills down my spine. When I was on my way back, I decided that I would never let any inconvenience get to me.

The reason for that is, I wanted to be grateful. I knew that I had survived the worst and that nothing worse could ever happen to me. This is why, as a sign of gratitude, I'd always be blessed and continue to count my blessings. I promised to remind myself that I survived a hurricane in the middle of the sea! And nothing can be more reason than that to always be filled with gratitude.

Despite my positive attitude, things kept getting tougher and tougher for me. The only thing that didn't seem to be falling apart was my finances. Which was now beginning to spiral out of control.

When my mother died, I got a fraction of the inheritance money – because it was split between all of us. My mother passed away in June 2017. Irma hit in September 2017. Those two were only months apart. I carried around the check with me for three months, till it finally went down with the boat. People asked me why I wasn't getting it cashed, and I didn't have an answer to give them.

My mother meant the world to me, and she just left. The pain and suffering were unbearable. Not just for me, but for all of us. I couldn't bring myself to spend that money because I was still grieving. So, I had it with me on the boat, the night that it sank. And at that moment, I knew how difficult it was going to be, getting that back.

From a legal standpoint, it seemed impossible. Because my mother had passed away, and there wasn't exactly anyone else authorized to take us through the procedure, all over again. It wasn't even about the money; it was about the amount of pain I was in. When I look back and think about everything, I can't help but call it the worst time of my life.

Losing a parent is hard enough, but I lost my father, then I lost my mother, then I lost my wife, and just when I thought it couldn't get worse, I almost died in a hurricane and lost the will to live. Speaking of my wife, our divorce had been finalized, and it all came down to the one thing it always comes down to – an equitable division of assets.

We ended up spitting everything equally. The only thing left to take care of was our townhouse. We had a bit of trouble with splitting that up, and there was a lot of going back and forth on it. Finally, both of us came up with a number, and she ended up buying me out of it. We made that decision mutually.

I didn't exactly like the idea of living in a big place all by myself, with my cats. I figured she'd be happy there, and I should let her have it. That's one of the things that surprises me the most – even my kids ask me this one thing, all the time. How have I managed to stay this calm through everything?

My answer always stays the same. I don't have it in me to wish anyone anything but the best. Even if it was my cheating ex-wife, I genuinely only want the best for her. I hope she's happy with whatever decisions she made for herself, and I hope she finds peace and comfort in the things she does.

I'm not sure whether or not she and her boyfriend are still together, but like I said, I wish her all the best. We were married for a few years, and it means something to me. I am my mother's son, and that's pretty much how she raised me. If she needs me, I'll try doing whatever I can in my capacity to be there for her.

Marriage isn't always natural, but it's still very special to me. I don't know if I ever see myself getting married again, but I'm sure I want to be on my own for a while.

During all of this, I was lucky I had insurance. As a shrimper, whenever your boat sinks and someone dies, there's always some sort of compensation. In our case, it was pretty sufficient since I had insurance. I wanted Carl's family to have all the money. I didn't even know how much money there was, but I had my lawyer send it to his family – all of it.

I was told that in most cases, it's enough to buy another boat. But in my situation, I didn't want to buy a boat or see another one, for what felt like the rest of my life. I couldn't imagine what Carl's family went through. I didn't even know how to face them. I loved Carl like a brother, and the trauma of losing him still feels fresh.

He was the best first-mate a man could ask for. I sometimes wonder if he's up there in heaven, looking down on me. I hope he doesn't feel let down in any way because there are times when I can't help but think that I could've saved Carl. Maybe it's my grieve, my guilt, or my conscience getting the best of me.

During everything that's been going on, I've learned a lot about life. I've learned that there are times when it'll feel like everything is falling apart, and the world is crashing at your feet. Everything happens in the blink of an eye, and it's so sudden that you won't even get the chance to process it. Or make peace with it.

But there's nothing to do, except to accept it.

To Carnival- the Miracle

Many people witness miracles in their lives while others do not believe in them. I did believe in miracles before it all happened, but I never expected to ever experience one myself. For others, Carnival might be a cruise ship, but the way I see it, it is a miracle in itself. Like I mentioned earlier, the odds of me surviving the storm were little to none. Carnival wasn't from Florida; it had come from the Bahamas as if it was destined to save my life.

Carnival not only pulled me out of the jaws of death but the way I was treated while I was struggling to cling to dear life; it made me realize that the existence of good people like those is keeping the world go. I find it funny how I have been using words like 'Miracle' and 'Survivor' lately. I never thought I could ever be a survivor or witness a miracle, but what can I say? There is no other way I can put it.

Sometimes in life, you get this sudden realization of everything you've endured and survived over the years. For me, it wasn't until after the storm that I realized just how much of a survivor I was.

The hurricane has been a real eye-opener for me. One event tested me beyond my strength and pushed my limits. After I'd weathered the storm, I began to think; I've endured so much more than just this hurricane. And that I most definitely was a survivor.

To be honest, my life is no 438 days – that's a fact. But that doesn't mean that I had it easy. I've been so used to all sorts of misfortune all my life that I guess I've just become immune to it. People believe that I take it well.

But for me, it's just something I never thought I'd do, but I ended up doing anyway because I wasn't left with much of a choice, unfortunately.

Surviving the hurricane and God's help in doing so made me acknowledge that I am true, a survivor. And it feels great to say that out loud – finally.

I used to think that I would never consider myself to be a survivor. Because I didn't know I was one. I just happened to be at the wrong place at the wrong time. And then I just got lucky.

God saved me. But I couldn't wrap my head around the idea of being called a survivor.

Now, I am told by many, including my children, that I have survivor skills and a warrior's soul. I laugh and say, 'I did what I had to.'

I still believe that I was tremendously lucky to be rescued on time. What if I was not found for some more time? I wouldn't have made it a week in the middle of the sea, all alone. With the trauma, the fear, the worry, the hopefulness, the hopelessness, and everything in between.

Whatever I have endured was too much, but it could have been worse, so one should always be grateful, as I am, for the miracle named Carnival.

It reminds me of one of the great memories with Carnival and the people associated with it. The crew contacted me that Captain G (Gaetano Gigliotti) was nominated for an award certificate for the miraculous rescue he and the crew had made to save me. The crew of the cruise ship Carnival Elation had been recognized with the Cruise Line Humanitarian Assistance Award from the Association for Rescue at Sea (AFRAS).

Carnival Cruise made the arrangements and paid for everything for me to fly to Washington State to witness Capt. Gigliotti receiving the award. They wanted me to be there. It was an emotional moment for me and, as far as I could feel it, for Captain G, as well.

Later on, I with my daughter, Jamie were flown down to London to watch him receive an international award. This was at the IMO in London, where I was even given a copy of the award received in Washington from the government. I was being awarded for my bravery, for my survival skills; I was really touched. I have the award copy framed at my house. I look at it sometimes and sigh; it always brings memories of Carl and Motorboat.

Just so you know, AFRAS is an organization that provides worldwide support and assistance to volunteer maritime rescue services and recognizes and honors extraordinary maritime rescues. Capt. G well deserved that honor.

When we went to London to attend the ceremony, Capt. G was being honored by IMO, which is International Maritime Organization. It was another feather in his cap. While in London, I and Capt. G did a podcast with BBC, and we were once again emotional as we re-lived those moments of panic and uncertainty. I will share the link to the podcast if any of you are interested in listening to it.

Now, I would love to include some background on the Carnival. Carnival Cruise Line is the world's most well-known cruise line, which was founded in 1972. The areas they mostly operate in include The Bahamas, Caribbean, Mexican Riviera, Alaska, Hawaii, Canada, New England, Bermuda, Cuba, Australia, New Zealand, the Pacific Islands, and Southeast Asia.

Along with their exceptional services, now they have the Humanitarian Assistance Award, too. During the whole situation and my rescue, every person on the crew was helpful and kind. Not just that, even after I came back home, they were amazing beyond words. If I used the term 'MIRACLE' for them, they very well live up to it.

The podcast can be found here: **https://www.bbc.co.uk/sounds/play/w3csw163**

The details of awards can be found online, as well.

My heart sinks whenever I think of the times, I avoided near-death experiences at sea. Ever since the hurricane, I've been continually trying to become a better person.

To never take life for granted. But at the same time, to expect the unexpected and always be prepared for whatever mother nature has to throw at you. That's the life of a fisherman. It's unpredictable and uncertain.

I can't even begin to imagine what would've happened to Marlene and Jamie if I had been missing longer than I did in the Bahamas. At the same time, I don't think being called a survivor should only be limited to surviving extreme natural disasters or a particular event. It can even consist of a consistent series of unfortunate events that some people call life.

Being a fisherman on a boat prepares you for a lot of things in life. I'd been on boats ever since I was 13 years old. I'd wanted to stay safe, in case of any and every emergency, I always wanted to be safe than sorry.

This is why I took classes on how to deal with sinking boats and CPR. But who knew that it'd all be put to the test in one single second? Hearing my partners voice saying;

"Eddie, we gotta go, we gotta go."

It just hit differently. No amount of words from the dictionary could ever describe the fear in his voice. It's something I'll never forget.

When you're on a 76-foot boat, there's a list of things that can go wrong, no matter how careful you are. Nothing in the world can prevent accidents from happening. And that's precisely what happened here.

No amount of safety training or precaution could've avoided what happened. It happened only because it was meant to happen. To this day, the thing that still shakes me to my core is; wondering why Carl didn't get into the water.

He warned me to get out in time; why wouldn't he even try to make it out in time? Did he freeze due to the shock and trauma of all that was happening around us? Or was he just afraid of the water? Why didn't he get on that raft when he could've easily made it?

There're a million questions I have, but I doubt I'm going to find the answer to any of them. That'll be tough luck. I've been shrimping in bad weather before. But even when worst came to worst, we were never in a situation like this.

But there is one thing that came out from all of this. It took time for me to accept and acknowledge it, but; I'm a survivor. Not because I survived Irma. But because I've been surviving life since forever now.

Carl and Motorboat

With everything that had been going on, I still made sure I remembered Carl and Motorboat from time to time. It's not something I did voluntarily, but something that came naturally. It hit all of a sudden, and it was always really intense.

Carl Shephard was my first mate on Capt. Eddie. We'd been working together for a while now, and I felt like we were family. When you happen to spend that much time with someone, it's obvious they're like family. Carl was family to me. He was a great man. He was kind, generous, he had a very good heart, and he was a man of God.

Carl was had been with me for a few years, and there are countless memories I have of that man. Since we were just a couple of regular dads and granddads, none of those memories is of the adventurous sort.

We were at a point in life where everything made sense, and it just felt good to slow down for a while and take each day as it comes. We'd spend a great time on the boat – hours would pass, and we'd realize how long it had been. Everything was always so relaxed with him; he was a natural.

Every time we'd be on the boat together, there isn't a single time that man didn't absolutely amaze me. Whether it was his political views or when he'd talk about God and his faith in God, for hours and hours, I could listen to him all day.

When I landed in Florida and saw my family after having just survived the hurricane, the news reporter asked me about Carl. I was already feeling very overwhelmed and extremely emotional. But hearing Carl's name, hit differently.

I knew he was gone, and that he wasn't coming back. But part of me couldn't accept that I'd lost my first mate and my friend. To make everything worse, the mention of him would always remind me of the time he died.

I'd play it back in my head, and I'd always beat myself over not being able to do enough to save him. He was a regular guy, just like me. We loved shrimping and being at sea. We always talked about our children and grandchildren. We were close, and it kills me that he isn't here with us today.

I couldn't stop thinking about his family. His wife and kids must have been going through hell, but again, there was nothing I could do. I wish I could've saved Carl. To be honest, I feel really ashamed at times. I was his friend, and it never occurred to me to ask him whether or not he was afraid of water.

I guessed when the time came, it was too late. Not knowing whether or not Carl was comfortable with the idea of getting into the water is something that always surprises me. I'd known him since ages – and it never occurred to me to find that out about him.

I guess in my defense, it's probably because you wouldn't usually consider believing a fisherman to be afraid of the water. Why would someone make a living doing what they fear? It baffled me. Even when it'd be a fun day, and we just wanted to cool down, he'd never swim.

I can't think of any of the reasons he'd given for not getting into the water ever, but I know that I couldn't remember any of them. Which makes me even more miserable than I was before.

Carl was the sole earning member of his family. With him gone, it worried me how his family would cope emotionally, and I feared they'd be in a rut financially. So, I spoke to my lawyer and figured out ways to help provide for his family.

Even though I never gathered the courage to go visit his family, I still keep him in my prayers every day. He was a big part of my life, and his death was a big part of the trauma and agony I endured over the years.

When I was interviewed at the airport after I landed in Florida, the news reporter asked me to say something about Carl, and I teared up. I didn't imagine a grown man like me would be tearing up on TV, but it happened.

So, I replied, "I love that man," and couldn't say more, unfortunately. Right off the bat, it was all that could come to my mind at that moment.

I had just seen my family after the worst days of my life. My soon to be ex-wife was confusing the hell out of me with her behavior. Cops surrounded the area where my family waited to greet me. It was all already very stressful, and I didn't know how much more of it I could take.

Carl was an extremely kind man with a heart of gold. His smile always lit up the room. Everyone who met him absolutely loved him. I was no exception. As his friend and colleague, I can safely say that I've never met anyone as kind as Carl.

I admired that he had family values and an outlook on life, which was very similar to mine. He placed his family above anything and everything, and the fact that he did just make me like him even more – even though I didn't think that was possible.

Carl was a very strong man. He was always smiling, no matter what life threw at him. I loved his spirit and admired his personality. He was one of those people who you refer to as 'a breath of fresh air' because he was just that.

He loved being in the ocean. He said that the ocean and open waters made him feel alive again – that they gave him a sense of belonging and brought him peace. It has been an incredible journey working with him and getting to know him. He was one of my best friends, and I cannot stress this enough; he was a *great* man.

Even though we'd spent so much time together, he'd still stick around for things that didn't even concern him. Which made me feel that he's just as fond of me as I am of him. Sometimes, we'd be shrimping for a whole day or two, and he'd still accompany me to the wheelhouse to get things done.

It always fascinated me. I don't even think my kids would want to see that much of me. I mean, I love my kids, and I'm pretty sure they love me, but everyone needs their space and their 'me-time.'

For him, me-time consisted of a few cold beers by the dock and us talking for hours. I'd like to add here that despite having a heart of gold, he was one of the most interesting and intellectual people I'd ever met.

His views on various subjects of politics fascinated me beyond belief. His faith in God made me want to be a better man. He was just always so learned about things. His opinions were strong, and he always made it a point to accept everyone's views and opinions with an open mind. No matter how contradictory they are to his own.

He was an incredibly patient man who I miss very dearly. He was a few years older than me, which is why people were partially skeptical about hiring him. To me, it was the best decision ever. To have known Carl and the amazing man that he is has been the highlight of my life.

I never got bored with Carl around. The man had so much knowledge, possibly everything and anything. He valued knowledge as if it was his prized possession. And to him, there was not a good time to learn something.

I'd seen him spend so much of his time reading books at the library, whenever we'd dock. There'd be an interesting, totally new book every time I saw him there. Each book would be worlds apart from the one before. He referred to that as 'broadening his knowledge horizon.'

He always spent his time at the library. If he wasn't reading a book, he'd be taking computer lessons. Like I said, he always wanted to keep learning. As an old man, he wanted to be up to date with technology, so that it never got the best of him. That's just the kind of man he was.

He never saw any shame in embracing your own shortcomings; in fact, he encouraged everyone to celebrate them because it makes people who they are. Carl was an exceptional man. He was kind, happy, and honest.

Honest, not just with his loved ones and those around him, but honest with himself and all of his hopes and dreams. I never got to know what they were, and it makes me regret every single day.

In my opinion, it symbolized strength, and Carl believed that change should always be valued – not criticized. Which is why he probably had such concrete faith, I believe. I hope someday I can be as steady and loving as Carl was.

Luckily, I ended up sorting things out with my lawyer, and we got our insurance company to give Carl's family the money I had been trying to. I haven't met with them ever since I made it back, and he didn't.

It just breaks my heart, and there's nothing I can do honestly. They say that God works in mysterious ways and that there's a bright side behind everything, but I cannot imagine what can possibly be the bright side here.

The man is gone forever. His children and wife are left alone in a world that isn't anything like the man he was. Carl's kindness was valued so much because kindness is rare – in today's day and time.

No matter how much we hate the fact, it is true. The world we live in today sucks. People are hitting new levels of low every single day. And as a human being, that worries me more and more every day.

As a dad, that terrifies me. But there's nothing I can do except to take each day as it comes and make the best out of life that I can. I know that by doing my part right, I'll be able to make a huge difference.

He was the kind of man; you can never forget. Working with him has taught me so much, I'm honestly glad I got the chance to get to know this incredible human being. I'm glad I hired him, and that he had a hard time finding work before me.

Because not only did I get an excellent resource in terms of work, I got a friend. A friend that I've always valued and cherished. And I intend to continue doing so for as long as I can. Even just the thought of him makes me happy.

I can't help but imagine what it'd be like if he was still here. We'd probably be close to retiring and finally making our way off the boat. But life had other plans for us, and that's okay. Sometimes, it's hard to believe that we'll never get to see him again.

There are days when I wish I could see him still riding his bicycle all over town. He had this bicycle that he loved to ride. He'd ride it for hours, and then when he got tired, he'd get off it and push it around.

God rest his soul in peace. He was a lovely man—one that I miss dearly and one that went away too soon. I pray for him every day, and I ask God to always bless his heart and give his family all the strength and courage they need.

As for Motorboat, he was the best pet I've ever had. I've been super attached to her for most of my life. Even though he was a present from my ex-wife, it never occurred to me that he was anything but mine.

I got along with her instantly, and we went on countless fishing trips. She was an amazing pet and a loving member of my family. Most days, it'd be just her and me at home. I spent most of my time with Motorboat.

Whether we were out at sea or at home just relaxing and laying back, it always felt great to be with her.

I have great memories of Motorboat. For the longest time that I can remember, it used to be just her and me. There were a couple of times when she fell off the boat, and I had to throw in a rope to the water to get her.

I'd take her out of the water and wash her in the sink with fresh water and dry her till she was warm and comfortable.

Those were the nights that she slept really well and long. I'm guessing it was because she was probably tired of swimming in the water.

I do miss Motorboat, more than I can actually explain. Motorboat was an excellent pet. She'd always listen to me.

She wasn't lazy like the other pets, and she was always up for an adventure. She was very attached to me, and I could tell she loved me very much. Like I said, there wasn't much to it; it was just her and me on most days.

It took me over seven months to get another pet. The trauma of losing Motorboat was a lot for me. I couldn't imagine getting another pet for as long as I remember.

Just the thought of it bothered me so much, it made my heart hurt. I felt responsible for Motorboat's death too. And that stayed with me for the longest time.

Dealing with the guilt of it all, and losing her right in front of my eyes, was all too much for me to take. The trauma of losing Motorboat, paired with the trauma of enduring the hurricane and going through my divorce, was what led to my depression.

There was a shelter I volunteered at a while ago. Seven months after Motorboat died, I went down there and adopted two brothers. They're with me now, and I've finally developed an emotional attachment with them.

I do miss Motorboat a lot, and I think about it all the time. Even though I'll never be as close to any other pet as I was with Motorboat, I still try to love my pets.

I dream about Motorboat from time to time, and I think about what I could've done to save her, but I realize now that nothing that I did could've changed what was meant to be. I know Motorboat is in a better place now, and I pray she's comfortable and looking down on me.

Faith and Spirituality

I've gone back and forth on this for a while now. But somehow, the answer I've found always brings me back to one thing, and one thing only. What is a person's real purpose in life? If you believe in God, you believe in everything God says.

It's obvious, and God created us for a reason. But what is that reason? Does it differ from person to person? What is my purpose? These are all the questions I've lately found myself focused on.

In my opinion, everything happens for a reason. Literally everything. Whether it was the fact that I set out to shrimp on the day of the hurricane, or that I got rescued, whether it was the fact that I got married or the fact that I got divorced – everything happened for a reason.

I've always heard people say that God works in mysterious ways. But I never truly understood the reason behind that statement, or even what it meant. All I know is that it might just be right. What that sentence means is that God works in ways that none of us can imagine. He always has a plan. And that plan is for the greater good.

It might seem like something corny, something that a happy or optimistic person might say, but I've recently found it to be very accurate indeed. Even though we may not realize it at the moment, God is, in fact, working in mysterious ways. Ways that are too grand and mighty to be comprehended by us.

The evidence for that can actually be seen in our lives. Almost all of us have gone through severe hardships at some point in our lives. And we've all been in a place where we were confident that nothing could work out. Even after we'd carefully evaluated the situation and went over every possible way to find a solution, nothing worked out. Until suddenly, out of nowhere, the entire predicament just disappears.

That is what I call divine intervention. Some people might not believe it, but the strength of your faith really makes a difference in your quality of life. Having strong faith is a great way to live, in my opinion. It just makes life so much better. You can't see God or hear Him, yet, we choose to believe in him. That basically means you have something great to look forward to in life.

In my case, I'd always been a relatively normal Christian man. My parents raised me to believe in God. And, as a child, whenever I'd question his existence, I never realized that He was around me all this time. In everything I do, in everything I see, God has always been all around me.

It usually takes some people to go through a drastic near-death experience to either restore their faith in God or to create it. It was a bit similar in my case. Not that my faith needed any restoration. But sometimes, life gets too busy, and we tend to lose sight of what's essential. Everyone is busy in this day and age, living their own fast-paced life. We often forget to slow down and just breathe.

We usually lose sight of what's important because we're focused on all the wrong things. We're always in such a rush to make it through the fast-lane, we barely even remember to ask our loved ones how they're doing. Kindness is a rare gem in today's world. And just because I've been blessed with some of the most helpful people doesn't mean everyone else would be too.

If you ever learned what was out there, you'd be surprised and shocked and sickened to your very core. I've lived the kind of life I never thought I'd be living. When I look back at some of my best years, there's so much I wish I could change. But at the same time, there's so much I wouldn't change for the world.

It's always a good thing to believe that everything happens for a reason. And that there's a bright side to everything. That's not just something naïve people think; it's actually true. It's all a matter of perspective.

When I got caught in the hurricane, I could've gone either way about it. I could've been pissed and thought that maybe God wanted me dead, which is why he scheduled for me to be at that particular time and place. And that I survived on my own. Or I could've believed that I happened to be at the wrong place in the wrong time and that if it wasn't for God, there's no way I would've made it through that night alive – Perspective.

I chose to believe that God made me survive for a reason. It was highly unlikely anyone in my state could've been rescued from the middle of the sea during an active hurricane. When Carnival came to rescue me, it was God's way of sending help. The funny thing about God sending help is that too many times, we don't even notice the help He sends, let alone appreciate it.

There's this hilarious story I've heard ever since I was a child. It went like; there was once a man who was drowning in the ocean. This man was a self-proclaimed man of God, with solid faith.

So, while he drowned, he kept praying to God to save him. A few minutes after, a boat of people came by and offered to help him up into the ship. He politely declined and claimed that he didn't need any help because God was going to save him. The people on the boat insisted, but eventually gave up and went away.

The man continued to drown. A little while after, another boat came by and offered to help him the same way – he declined their help, again. And continued to drown. Not too long after that, a rescue helicopter flew right above him and lowered a ladder for him to hang on to and climb.

The man declined the rescue team's help too. Apparently, he kept telling everyone that God would save him, which is why he declined everyone's help. Hours passed by, and his arms got tired of flailing around, his body started to feel weak. He finally drowned. When he asked God why He didn't save him, God told him that he tried to save him by sending help several times. But he declined the help.

Even though it's obviously a humorous anecdote, there's still a valuable lesson in it. God won't personally come down and help you through all your hardships in life. Instead, he'll send people to help you. If you accept His help, those people will most likely end up becoming your saving grace.

For me, it was the captain at Carnival. He is one of the nicest people I've ever met. I can't imagine where I'd be today if it weren't for him. That man saved my life, literally. And for that. Nothing I do or say could ever show him how grateful I am.

I still keep in touch with him. We often talk on thanksgiving, Christmas, and other holidays or birthdays. He's like family to me. Captain Gaetano Gigliotti was the best thing to ever happen to me, even during a hurricane.

I'm sure his parents are proud of what a fine man they've raised. He truly is one of a kind. And it's not just because he rescued me. It's everything else too. From the moment he and his team rescued me, till the moment I got off the boat in Freeport, they'd been nothing less than incredible and exceptional. I mean every word of that.

For me, he was indeed a Godsent. An angel in disguise. I believe that I was meant to be where I was when the hurricane hit. And I also think that God planned it that way because he wanted me to know that I still got a lot of good years ahead of me.

When Wesley's son was comforting Wesley about not knowing where I was, he asked his dad not to worry because God would surely be taking care of me. He is such a fine young man, very wise for his age.

He didn't even know where I was and whether or not I was alive, but he still had enough faith in God. Enough to comfort his father and reassure him that his brother would be back. Now that is what I call unshakable faith.

The words that really stuck with me were, "God can move mountains, have faith in Him. Uncle Eddie will come home". Even to this day, the more I think about it, the more it fascinates me. I get goosebumps every time.

God really did move mountains for me to make it out of the hurricane alive. That giant ship that came to my rescue was just Him moving mountains to make everything work for me. And anyone who knew the condition of the storm and how rough the waters were that night knows that someone couldn't climb onto a ladder so high, from a life raft.

Every second that goes by reminds me of how grateful I am to have God's love and support in my life. Sometimes I wonder what I ever did right. Maybe He's just like that – perhaps He's just incredibly giving and gracious.

One of my favorite things to do when I'm feeling low is to count my blessings. It just sets everything into perspective, and it shapes your entire thought process. I never really believed this before, but having a positive outlook in life is rewarding.

My strategy has lately been pretty straightforward. Instead of focusing on what I don't have and what didn't work out, I simply focus on what I have and what fortunately did work out. For instance, whenever I think about either of my ex-wives, I want to figure out where everything went wrong. And why it couldn't work out with anyone of them.

I think about the times I was immeasurably miserable and that I could've done this with someone else. Maybe I would've ended up a lot happier. I try to not focus on the negatives like the fact that I wasted more than a decade trying to find the right person.

Again, there are two sides to everything. And in even the worst situations, you can find the good if you just tried to. For me, the good in my failed marriages; were my children. Marlene, Eddie, and Jamie. My children mean the world to me.

The fact that they think of me as a good father and love me enough to always be there for me is a massive accomplishment for me. It means that I obviously must've done something right for these kids to turn out the way they did – exceptional.

As I said, everything is God's plan. We're all a part of it. Everyone gets their chance to shine at some point in their life, and you just need to have faith. For me, I'll admit it was very hard. The hurricane was just the beginning of it, unfortunately.

Because everything that came after the hurricane is what was a long and painful process. The rescue took a couple of hours at most. But what followed after that is what emotionally, mentally, physically, and financially drained me for months and months.

As I said, I've always wanted to keep a positive outlook towards life, but sometimes it just gets hard. We all have our bad days, and that's okay. The critical thing to remember is that it's never too late – to trust God to do His job.

If you feel like you're entitled to more than what you currently have, then don't give up just yet. Your time is coming; you just need to believe it. And if you'd like for it to happen sooner than later, the easiest thing to do is; to count your blessings. Constantly be grateful for them and always find the good in the bad.

Life, Then and Now

After a lot of back and forth on whether or not I was going to ever buy a boat again, I decided not to. I have countless reasons for why it didn't seem like a good idea, but for me, the only thing that convinced me not to do it was my peace.

I wanted to remember that part of my life in good times. I didn't want to associate shrimping or being on a boat with Irma; in fact, I wanted it to be a good memory that I could look back on. I'd always loved my boat. I'll never forget the feeling when I first got on it and how happy I felt.

People have their favorite things in life; they aim to accomplish a certain material goal or wealth. For some, it's a car, a house, and for some, it's a trip or a milestone in their career. For me, it had always been my boat – Capt. Eddie.

My boat was named after my son, Eddie. I loved calling it Captain Eddie. Made me feel like the king of the world or the captain of the sea in this case. I spent my entire life on that boat, and if I had to, I'd do it again – given that the hurricane never existed.

After all that happened, I believe that I'm in a really good place in my life right now. I'd like to think that I'm more stable, more together, and that everything in my life has finally started to make sense to me. Whether it was the hurricane, my divorces, or losing all the people that I lost. I've learned to make peace with life – the good and the bad.

One thing that I still struggle with from time to time is; I sometimes drift away. I don't have much to do, but I'm a thinker, so it makes time go by faster than I realize. The thing with people who think is that they tend to feel everything. And not just feel it, but feel it a bit too much. I've never considered myself a sensitive guy, but when I think about it, I believe that I am.

It doesn't necessarily mean that I'm a weak or a soft person but that I have a different perspective about life than the rest. Life wasn't made for us to just live it or for it to pass by. We were brought into this world to make something of ourselves and to leave our mark.

The people who have been a part of our lives should feel like you made their world go round. After you've left your mark on this world, after you've lived, and you've loved, comes the tricky part.

As cliché as it sounds, I would love to know what people say about me. I would love to know how much of a difference I made in which a person's life. Whether it was either of my daughters, my ex-wife, or my best friend. Knowing how much I meant to them would be the only way for me to calculate how well I lived my life.

Not that I fear that I'm going to die anytime soon, but I do think about death a bit. Maybe a bit more than before ever since the hurricane. It was night; I just can't forget. It's going to stay with me forever. That's the worse part. Whether I like it or not, it'll always stay with me.

No matter how hard I try to forget about it, I won't let myself forget. And people are going to always want to know how it felt and what I went through until they don't. People get tired, and pretty soon, everything seems like a stunt for attention. Trauma, pain, and scars are expected to heal with time.

But what people don't realize is that it takes so much more than just time to heal. It takes emotional support, professional help, lots of love, encouragement, patience, strength, prayers, and long sleepless nights. But people have this preconceived notion that 'time' is all it takes to heal.

So, you're basically expected to sit there and do nothing. Nothing but to expect time to heal all wounds and make everything right. And when it takes all of your patience, strength, and sleepless nights, and you finally start to heal, time is given credit for it all.

So, in my life, everyone finally began to see that I was healing. It took months and months of professional help, failure to inspire myself, failure to love myself, constant faith in God, constant struggle to succeed, and a ton of self-doubt.

But again, all everyone believed was that it took time. And that even without all my efforts and help, if I would've just waited it out, it would've been alright in the end.

This mindset is beyond me. I don't understand what it takes for some people to show a little gratitude or to appreciate someone. In all honesty, I might have not understood the whole idea of it either, until I finally realized how much it could mean to someone.

The world we live in today is full of people who don't think twice before telling someone off, and they don't realize what it's like for the other person. That's the worst part.

Just because I was blessed with a few good people in life, doesn't mean everyone else is too. And lately, ever since I've been on my own, I've been thinking a lot about life – and its complexities. I can't help but think that there's so much in life that we try to change, and there's so much in life, that there's no way we can change.

When it comes down to the hurricane, I don't regret a thing. In fact, I feel like it made me who I am today, many years after I thought I was done finding myself. I've learned that there will always be certain situations where God wants to put your strength to the test and see how far you can go.

In my case, I didn't realize that at first, but now that I do, it makes everything so worth it. Every time my children tell me that they look up to me for the level of strength and patience I possess, I'm amazed. My heart fills with gratitude, and I can't help but thank God for allowing me to be someone that my children can look up to.

Now, things are looking great for me. I don't have a wife and decided not to go down that road again for a while, possibly ever again even. And I can safely say that it's for the best. Marriage is something people enter into with their hearts full of love and a bond formed on everlasting promises meant to be honored.

If people got married, just for the hell of it, even animals would have spouses, and that's ridiculous. So, there's one reason I'm done with marriage for good this time. I can't be ungrateful, and if I'm completely honest, I've had a pretty great run.

Even though all my marriages ended in divorce, they were still the best thing to ever happen to me. Two of my ex-wives gave me the most beautiful children in the world, and nothing is above that – everything in the world is such a reward.

Which means I can safely say that I've loved learning from life. I've loved taking and accepting all the wisdom and lessons life has had to offer over the past several years. The only part I wish I could be that I wish I could realize everything sooner.

Usually, when I'm in such a tricky situation, I often tend to blame it on life's surprises, and I feel out of place for something so unfortunate happening to me. But with time, I've learned to realize that everything happens for a reason. And ever since I've applied that theory to my perspective, my life is a *whole lot* better.

I just learned to accept the fact that everything happens for a reason and that I'm supposed to take the good with the bad, no matter what. The other day, I was reading this very interesting article on a gospel website; it's primarily what shaped and solidified my belief and perspective.

The conversation was about a man complaining to God about all the unfortunate instances that occurred with him in just a single day.

Man: Why did You let so much bad stuff happen to me today?

God: What do you mean?

Man: Well, I woke up late...

God: Yes.

Man: My car took forever to start, and I JUST got a new battery.

God: Okay.

Man: At lunch, they made my sandwich all wrong, and I had to wait.

God: Hum...

Man: On the way home, just as I picked up a call, my phone went DEAD.

God: All right.

Man: And on top of it all off, when I got home, I just wanted to soak my feet in my new foot massager and relax. But it wouldn't work! Nothing went right today! Why did You do that to me?

God: Let me see... this morning, the angel of death was at your bed, and I had to send one of My Angels to battle him for your life. I let you sleep through that.

Man: (humbled) Oh...

GOD: I stopped your battery for a bit because there was a drunk driver on your route that would have hit you if you were on the road.

Man: (ashamed said nothing)

God: The first person who made your sandwich today was sick, and I didn't want you to catch what they have, so I ripped the bread; I knew you couldn't afford to miss work.

Man: (embarrassed) Okay...

God: Your phone went dead because the person that was calling was going to give false witness about what you said on that call; I didn't let you talk to them so you'd be protected.

Man: (softly) I see God.

God: Oh, and that foot massager? It had a shortage that was going to throw out all of the power in your house tonight. I didn't think you wanted to be in the dark.

Man: I'm sorry, God.

God: Don't be sorry, just learn to Trust Me in All things, the Good and the bad

Reading this was a real eye-opener for me. It made me realize that even though things don't always go my way, God is always looking down on me. It's the reason why Irma suddenly doesn't seem like a big deal anymore, and why I've accepted that it was all part of the plan. And that if it wasn't for that night, I could've ended up in a much worse place.

But God intended for me to be okay, and so I was – alive and kicking till this day! His faith in me has restored all my self-doubts and steered away from my fear of failure. I try to constantly be the best version of myself, as much as I can. I strive to be a man of God, a loving father, a good friend, a caring brother, and a good human being.

Even though life is pretty simple now due to the current situation, I still try not to remember things that I'm not supposed to. I try to take care of myself and take each day as it comes. I bought my daughter out of the house we bought together since she and her husband were moving to a bigger house.

I miss Motorboat, and it took me a while before I could emotionally invest in another pet, but I did. I now have two cats, named Shephard and Sadler. They're both named after two of my crew members that passed away. I thought of naming one of them after Carl, but I couldn't bring myself to do that. It'd be too much, and it would've just made forgetting very hard, I believed.

I travel several times a year, sometimes, several times a month. I see my children and grandchildren, at least once a month, regularly. Unless something comes up and they need my help with something. Or if it's a special event, which I didn't know of for now.

I miss the boat and fishing, but I'm completely okay with never having to own one again. I've been out with my son Eddie on the boat fishing for quite a few times ever since the hurricane. And I have to say, I actually enjoyed it.

Do I miss it? Maybe a little. But do I miss is enough to start over and relive that trauma? I don't think that would be the best idea in the world.

Jamie's Epilogue

There is something very surreal about talking to someone you love, which is completely healthy and capable, but knowing you might never speak to them again. They might die, and everything you are telling them at that moment might be the last time you ever speak to them. No illness or disease is taking them down; this wasn't something you saw coming. They sound fine on the phone; you just physically can't get to them or save them. It makes your words and your feelings turn into something new. Something you never knew could be possible. I don't wish that feeling on anyone.

Hurricane Irma was coming to Florida. As a Floridian, I'm so used to this warning. I was born in the Keys and spent nearly all of my life in Florida. Every Hurricane season, they say the Tampa Bay area is due for a major storm, and we prep, and we buy canned food and batteries like good Floridians. Hurricane Irma looked threatening, so we all prepped a little more than normal. My Dad was on his boat down in the Keys, and I called him about a week before the storm was supposed to arrive. When we first spoke, he said he was going to take the boat back home to Tarpon Springs. I called him again a few days later, and he changed his mind. At that time, he said he and a hand full of other boats were going to tie up behind Ft. Jefferson to ride out the storm. Now, this is a very normal thing for fishermen.

Key West doesn't much care for the big shrimp boats to be tied up at their docks during hurricanes because they knock around the wealthy people's yachts. I'm not judging Key West on this; it's just good business.

Essentially there was no room to tie up at the docks, and my Dad's boat, a 75ft commercial boat, was no speed boat. Getting to Tarpon would have cost thousands in fuel and a solid day plus of travel. Irma was also supposed to go up the east coast of Florida and just graze Key West. Ft. Jefferson is also miles from Key West. When I spoke to my Dad, and he said he made this decision, I asked him two things; first, did you keep your insurance? Second, are there still other boats with you? With his boat paid off, he technically didn't need to carry insurance, and he told me a few years before that he had considered canceling it because it had gotten so expensive. He said yes, he had kept it. Secondly, he confirmed there were about eight other boats with him, hiding behind the Fort.

My Dad and I had the little house in Holiday, Fl for about eight years at that point. With the cheapest mortgage payments, my husband and I had decided to stay there and try to pay off debts and save as much money as possible. However, Holiday is prone to flooding and is very close to the coastline. We had cleaned up the house, put out sandbags, lifted everything about three feet off the ground, unplugged everything, took photos of our belongings for insurance. We were planning for the possibility that our home might be flooded. We were planning for the possibility of our home being destroyed, but I had never planned on the possibility my Dad might die.

We packed up our documents and cats and went to my Mother's house in Trinity, Fl. Trinity is much more inland and figured they wouldn't have any issues. In the great luck of the draw, her A/C unit died about two days prior, and with the storm coming, no one would come out and fix it. So, with four people, now three cats, a four-bedroom house, we were all living in the guest bedroom because my Mom's boyfriend Scott put in a window shaker, so that was the only cool room in the house. I spent the day helping Scott put up plywood over the sliders. My Mother's house has five sliding glass doors and an obscene number of windows, so it was no small task. We took a break after a few hours, and I decided to call my Dad just to check-in; the storm would be at the Keys at that time, still nearly a day away from us in Trinity.

When I called my Dad's satellite phone, I was greeted with a flow of words. I couldn't really understand everything that was being said to me, so after a few minutes, I asked, "Dad?" I thought maybe the lines were crossed; it sometimes happens with storms coming. It was from Carl. Carl had a tendency to talk fast, and with his accent, I couldn't always understand him. Sat phone connections aren't usually crystal clear either. Carl then took a breath, slowed his words, and tried to repeat himself. He told me, "Jamie, we're taking on water. Coast guard can't help. We're in a really bad place, Jamie, we're in a really bad place." And with that, I dropped to my knees in my Mom's patio and tried to digest what I just heard. Knowing Carl was older and had some injuries, I knew my Dad was the one working to keep the boat afloat.

There was no point in asking to speak to him because that would cost him time fixing the boat and cost Carl pain from having to climb down into the engine room where I assumed my Dad was. Physically I was shaking, crying tears without actually crying; I couldn't form words as my thoughts were too jumbled. I told Carl to remind my Dad I loved him and that I'd call back.

I hung up the phone and was shaking horribly, my Mom came out and asked what happened, and I told her my Dad was sinking. My husband came to me and was rubbing my arms and saying something to me as I just stood there, shaking. I don't know what anyone said to me for the next few minutes. I'm ashamed to say that I didn't have pretty much any family members' phone numbers so, I got on Facebook. I was asking if anyone knew someone in the Keys with a boat.

If anyone could help. This was when my Dad's wife of the time called me. She told me she had just spoken to my Dad, that he was fine and that I was scaring the family. At this point, she had already cheated on my Dad, moved in with a boyfriend, and the fact she said "family" sent me into a rage. In my eyes, she was no longer allowed to mention my family. Let alone tell me to stop being concerned for my Dad. I told her off, screamed at her, called her every name I could think of because for the last year or so, I had already been referring to her as the devil woman.

This was long before the divorce process started. I wasn't a big fan. To me, she was and always will be manipulative, belittling, greedy, and vain. However, I was now so exhausted from packing up my house, helping prep my Mom's, hearing my Dad might be sinking, yelling at this woman that I had to lay down. I was also in the process of changing jobs. The mental and physical drain was too much for me.

My Mom, Julie Potter, went to the neighbor's house. They had a family member in the coast guard, so she was trying to figure out who we could contact. Her boyfriend, Scott, was still working on prepping the house but had decided to help me as well. When I got up, I checked my phone immediately, and there was a missed call from an unknown number. Sat phones tend to show up as unknown or private numbers. When I played the message, I was brought back to reality quickly. My Dad had called, and his message was, "Jamie, we've uh got some serious problems. Call me back, I love you." Weirdly, I was hoping the soon to be ex was right. Maybe Carl was exaggerating; maybe it wasn't that bad.

Maybe I am reading too much into this. No. I realized in the time it took a voicemail to play, that I was going to have to do everything I was capable of to help my Dad, 250 miles away. This was a call to arms, and my family and I answered. I called my Dad and spoke to him briefly. Half yelling through the static of the sat phone and half sobbing, I told him he can't go down with the boat. Scott was in the background, asking for coordinates.

My Dad told me they wouldn't be able to send a chopper out until the next day because of the storm. Key West Coast Guard had been evacuated, so they were in Miami. When I asked if he thought the boat could hold out that long he wasn't sure. My Mom and Scott found the number for the Miami Coast Guard, and that became our new favorite speed dial. Giving coordinates, asking for updates, asking anything we could. My Dad confirmed they had the lifeboat inflated and ready, tied up on the side just in case.

The Coast Guard informed us there was a cruise ship in the area, and they were going to try to have them pick up Carl and my Dad. I don't think there are words to explain how ridiculous that seemed. My Dad has had boat problems before. He's had the engine die. He's had to be towed back to the docks. These are normal things about owning a boat. In any other time, he would have called another fisherman, or the Coast Guard, had some pumps dropped off to empty out the engine room and been towed home.

This was a simple thing that should have been. But there was Irma, she threw a wrench in the process. No one was there to help, but a cruise ship. I mean seriously, a cruise ship.

My sister Marlene found me on Facebook. Luckily, she's much closer to the family and had nearly everyone's phone number. I didn't grow up around most of my family, so it was the once every two-year vacation visits. I can say this disaster has brought me much closer to most of my family, and that's a blessing.

Marlene was like a beacon of hope for me. Someone I could talk to that cared just as much as I did, and she kept me sane. I think I survived on alcohol and nicotine for about two weeks straight, but she stayed up and talked with me, and she talked to the family and gave everyone updates. After a few hours of talking to the Coast Guard and talking to my Dad, everything went silent. This is when Marlene just listened to me for several hours. We didn't know for sure what was happening. We were hoping it meant Dad and Carl were picked up from the cruise ship, but really, we knew nothing.

We finally got the Coast Guard to tell us the cruise ship did, in fact, pick up my Dad. They said they got one. Not two people. One. The dread that hit my stomach was like a rock or a boat sinking in the Gulf. They said it was Edward Potter, my Dad. However, we had no way to know. We had no way to be certain. I can't thank the Coast Guard and my family enough. I know it was the countless phone calls being made that coordinated this rescue.

I know it was the bravery and mastery of the cruise ship captain, Capt. G. I know there was so much bad that happened, but so much good had to happen at the same time to bring my Dad home. With that being said, the Coast Guard and the cruise ship were very tight-lipped on anything. There were never details. There were never hopes or promises. It was a very matter of fact and literally all facts. Marlene and I figured out that we couldn't ask open-ended questions. Everything had to be to the point.

The Coast Guard, probably sick of dealing with every Potter in the United States, gave me the email address to the cruise ship. Realizing we had to be plain in our questions, I asked specifically about the crewman; I didn't want to use Carl's name. If they gave me the name, that would mean the person on board would have given it and was coherent. I then asked if the person on board would be capable of making it to dock without any assistance.

Marlene agreed to stay up with me until I got the response back. The email I got back stated they were sorry for the loss of Carl and Motorboat (my Dad's cat) and that yes, my Dad would be able to make it to dock. With that, I finally texted Marlene and told her it was confirmed, our Dad was safe, and we could both attempts to sleep. Not knowing what happened to Carl but too exhausted to pry any further.

Waking up the next morning was like waking up from a nightmare. Everything that had happened seemed so impossible, but at least our Dad was safe. We didn't know the details. We just knew our Dad was coming home. We didn't know Capt. G had pulled off a miracle by blocking the 15-20 feet waves from my Dad in his lifeboat. We didn't know that they had already searched every other grid trying to find him.

We didn't know my Dad has spent at least an hour in a lifeboat alone. We didn't know he had lost his cat and sat phone when the lifeboat popped up and nearly drowned him. We didn't know he had to climb 20 feet of the rope ladder to get into the cruise ship. We didn't know what happened to Carl and that he never jumped into the water to get to the raft. We didn't know what my Dad's soon to be ex-wife had gone to the docks and told everyone, including our family, that Carl and my Dad both made it. No, we didn't know any of it.

Marlene had the unfortunate job of telling our Uncle Wesley that Carl didn't make it. Trying to undo the damage she had done. I understood then why the cruise ship and the Coast Guard were so tight-lipped. Only the facts. Don't give anyone useless hope. Because it's a crushing blow to rip it away. The Coast Guard did later do a search to find Carl. The only thing they found was the lift raft, which they shot down.

Another thing we didn't know is the cruise ship was headed to the Bahamas. Most cruise ships are based out of

Miami, so I was assuming one of us would drive down to pick up Dad. I really wasn't excepting to still be fighting to get him back home. The cruise ship informed me they were going back to Freeport. At this point, there was a direct line we had to Carnival Cruise. There was a "relations" person we were speaking to. God bless that man because he had to deal with a lot of questions. Because now that my Dad was no longer in the water, the Coast Guard was out of it.

I jokingly thought of telling my Dad to jump off the cruise ship because that might be the only way we could bring him home! He was in a foreign country, with no money, no identification, no passport. So, the first step was speaking to the Embassy to get him some ID. Luckily my Dad had gotten a passport a few years back, so they were able to start the process of expediting one. Since I had taken my documents to my Mom's house, I had papers with his social security number on them, so I was able to provide that.

I forgot he was a junior, so it took them a while to match him up. Marlene later told me she had given her month of birth instead of his when booking his flight, so we were all of our sorts. It made me feel better knowing it wasn't just me. We were all in new territory.

You would think it would be so simple, the cruise ship docks, and they take him to the Embassy. Well, the Bahamas is not like the US, where you can just drive somewhere. The Bahamas is a string of islands, and you need to take a boat or plane to get to Nassau (where the Embassy is) from Freeport (where the cruise ship docked.)

The cruise ship was undergoing a makeover, and I've seen pictures of it now that it's finished and it looks beautiful. This wonderful woman named Barbara Wallace was our point of contact at the Embassy. Talking to her, you'd think she handles these situations every day. She was so calm, so helpful, and I just can't thank her enough for everything she did. She informed me that there was a mail boat that would come on Thursday and could have him dropped off at the Embassy by Saturday.

When I called Carnival back, I asked if they could house him for that long? Well, apparently, liability issues were a motivating factor because next thing I knew, they had a team escorting my Dad to an airport to get him to Nassau.

When someone is undocumented and has no money in another country, most people don't want to take on the liability. When I had first spoken to Barbara Wallace, she informed me that a plane would be ridiculously expensive because he would need to pay for all the seats that weren't filled. Essentially it would be a private charter. Plus, you can't fly without ID.

Apparently, Carnival covered the cost of it because this strange fisherman with no money or ID was a bit of a risk on a ship being renovated. It's actually pretty funny if you think about it. I was thinking we were going to be waiting a week on a mail boat because the planes wouldn't let him fly. It got to the point whenever I had to ask if ID was required, I'd just give them Barbara Wallace's phone number, and she'd work some sort of magic, and it would get done.

To get the physical passport to get him back in the states, though required money and a new photo. Carnival arranged a car to take him to get a photo and dropped him off at the Embassy. I booked him a hotel across the street because the flight to Tampa wasn't going to be until the next day. He got his passport, thanks to Uncle Wesley, sending him some money through Western Union (thanks to my cousin Andrew for doing it online) and got himself some dinner. Unfortunately, I didn't think that I just used my credit card in a foreign country, so they declined the charge canceled my card for fraud. So, my Uncle got wrapped up again.

I had a Southwest card, so I was planning on flying him through that, but Marlene was nice enough to cover the flight home just to get him on the next flight to get him home as soon as possible. I was finally able to talk to my Dad when he was in the hotel room. He told me he called his soon to be ex-wife and told her he was coming home the next day. I didn't want to rock the boat or let him know all the damage she had done.

I later asked why he had called her instead of Marlene or me on anything; he told me her number, and Uncle Wesley's were the only ones he knew by heart. He had already filed for divorce, but I think he just needed someone to talk to. Anyone would do, even the person who had just hurt him.

My sister and I arrived at the airport, my Uncle Wesley and Uncle Kevin flew in to be with my Dad as well. It was so nice of everyone to come to support him. My brother, Eddie, had evacuated and would spend some time with him later on when everyone else had cleared out some. There were reporters everywhere as my Dad's soon to be ex-wife had contacted them. We were working to move them back when my Dad arrived. In shoes with no socks, reading glasses he could hardly see out of, a tourist Bahamas shirt, and a pair of swim trunks with turtles on them, he walked through the gates.

There was a sense of relief seeing him, finally, and knowing concretely, he was okay. What we didn't know yet again was the biggest danger. None of us could prepare for the mental and emotional issues he was going to struggle with for months and honestly, even to this day.

After he first arrived, we went back to his townhouse in Tarpon Springs, and he told us about all the things that happened that we didn't know about. It was heartbreaking and exhausting for him, but we wanted to listen and understand. Reporters were calling, attorneys calling, insurance agents, Coast Guard. It was nonstop, and he wasn't really capable of these decisions just yet. I would talk to my Dad every day, sometimes multiple times a day. We all did. Check-in phone calls. Then we'd report back to each other on status.

There were times he'd repeat himself three or four times in one thirty-minute phone call. I'd get off the phone with him crying, thinking something in my Dad had broken, that couldn't be recovered. He lost so much in such a short period. His Mother, marriage, boat and livelihood, his dear friend Carl and his cat Motorboat. Living with the survivors' guilt is still something he struggles with. Still thinks of things he could have done differently. Still obsesses over it sometimes. We've all gone over the story with him enough times to know there was nothing different that could have been done. However, we talk it out with him, hoping it'll help him heal. Physically he was sore, he was run down, dehydrated, but mentally it took a lot longer to bring him back.

I don't know if a person ever fully recovers from something like this. He feels responsible for the boat and everybody and animal on board. If any other day, without a hurricane, this would have been another expensive tow trip, and that's all. When Marlene and I were talking, I told her I feared this from when I was a little kid. She told me she never did; she knew he was too capable and smart to ever end up in this situation.

With a great family and great support system, he's doing much better today. There were so many things that helped to bring this story into a happy ending for at least my family. It's far from a happy ending for everyone, though.

My Dad started volunteering at the local SPCA shortly after doing a family visiting tour. I had taken him with me on a day of errands that included dropping off some supplies at the SPCA and going to the used book store. I asked if he wanted to come along to get out of the house and play with some kittens.

He stayed there for several months doing laundry and cleaning up and then ended up adopting two brother kittens. We convinced him to go to therapy for a bit, which he did. I'm still working on getting him a hobby other than the movie theaters, but he did agree to get a kayak and seems to enjoy that from time to time.

For someone who's business, identity, income, hobby, friends, everything in life, was a boat that is now in the middle of the ocean floor, he's adjusting better than most. I'm so grateful he's had the opportunity to do this book because I think it allows him to thank those that deserve it, mourn for Carl's loss, and get a therapy secession essentially out of it. I will never be able to thank Capt. G from Carnival Cruise enough who I had the pleasure of meeting in London when he received an award for bravery at sea. Such a humble man, who explained in great detail the maneuvering he had to do to rescue my Dad.

The way he spoke about his crew and how overjoyed they were to be able to do a rescue, he's an amazing person who loves his career and crew very much. It's something those men/women will never forget. They will never know the joy they gave back to our family, though. In a recording, you can hear one of them say, "Okay, Captain, work your magic" as soon as they saw the small light beacon of the life raft. It was magic.

Barbara Wallace is forever one of those people who, like my sister Marlene, helped me stay sane when it seemed like the world was falling apart at the seams. The entire Embassy and Carnival were such a well-oiled machine you really would think this was just a normal day for them. The Coast Guard, who fielded countless phone calls from our entire family and organized an entire cruise ship to come search for my Dad. The insurance agencies, the attorneys, there was even one reporter that helped us get the others in line to not shock my Dad when he arrived.

I can honestly say I only met Carl a couple of times. Everyone loved him, and my Dad truly admired his motivation to learn, his passion for his beliefs, and his ability to talk such highly debatable things like religion and politics with a calm head and faith. My Dad once told me he taught himself how to read by visiting the library and became an avid reader. He seemed like a wonderful person and was taken away too quickly by the sea.

My Dad also told me Carl was very scared of getting in the water. Carl even mentioned, "what if there were sharks?' My Dad's response was, "if there are sharks, it's just our time to go. We can't worry about sharks." I've asked before if Carl could swim, and no one seems to know the answer for sure. All I can say it's I'm so sorry for his family, like the rest of us. We would all be happy to have everyone home with us. Unfortunately, it didn't happen that way. I'm so sorry for what Carl's family went through, and I know the horror as we were going through the same thing. The only thing I can do is be grateful and know how lucky I am that we got my Dad back. Dad to three and Grandpa to five.

He's enjoying the grandparent's life, and I'm happy to have him for a Dad. Thank you, Dad, for coming home to us. Even though it took a toll on you. We are glad to have you back on land, dealing with land people's problems.

Marlene's Epilogue

It's hard to recount the events of hurricane Irma. When I think back on it, everything that happened seems surreal and so sequential that I find myself saying thank God I did that. When my dad was finally safe in the Bahamas, I sat down to write the events of what had happened, so it didn't all turn into a blur.

It did anyway.

Now upon rereading the events and thinking back to how it all played out there are some things that stand out more than others, that at the time didn't seem so critical.

I typically wait to hear from my dad before I prepare for a storm. He's a master at the weather and when hurricane chaos floats through my school (I'm a teacher) and the grocery stores, even in my house with my husband I wait to hear from my dad.

I remember my friend Bonnie asking me if I was prepared for IRMA or preparing, I told her I didn't really get ready until I heard from my dad...which later would be a really weird memory.

I usually don't speak to my dad when he's shrimping, waiting to hear from him every time he was back at the dock. His satellite number sat on the bar in my house, for about a month, until I threw it out because I never needed to call him on it. I had his cell number and when he was in or close to shore that number worked fine.

When Irma rolled in and I hadn't heard from my dad, I called his cell phone with no answer, only voicemail. I was not close with my dad's then wife. Calling her was out of the question. So, I called my uncle Wesley in North Carolina. He and my dad are close and I figured he would have heard from him.

My Uncle said he'd heard from my dad and he was anchoring up off of Fort Jefferson. I spent many young summers shrimping with my dad on the Capt. Eddie and I know Fort Jefferson, at Dry Tortugas. That area holds good memories for me of vacation when my parents were together. We would take Capt. Eddie there for a summer vacation, to swim and snorkel. I'd often thought it would be a place my dad would eventually take my kids for a vacation. On the same boat I went there on.

Irma took that away.

So, Uncle Wesley told me my dad was safe, anchored up at Fort Jefferson, I told my uncle I'd had my dad's satellite number, but had thrown it out. I was hesitant to ask for it because I was not really on speaking terms with my dad's current wife, and it seemed like everyone liked her but me. However, Wesley said he had the number if I wanted it, and at first I declined, but then I said I'd better take it thinking I would never use it.

I spoke to my uncle Wesley a second time and he relayed that my dad had to pull anchor and was running west because he didn't feel comfortable at Fort Jefferson. I felt comfortable with that, secure in my dad's ability to captain his boat and understand the weather. He'd been doing it for (in my calculations) about thirty-eight years.

I decided to call my dad for myself. Not sure why, but I remember hanging up with my uncle after hearing my dad was on the move and decided that I would just check in on him.

That was at 1:00, I believe on Thursday or Friday Sept. 7 or 8th. All this conversation happened on my house phone so I really have no time stamp record of it.

In my notes I have the conversation written line for line.

Carl answered the phone and I thought it was dad.

Here's the conversation line by line....

Me: Dad?

Carl: This is Carl, Eddie's not up here.

My dad shouts from the background: Who is this?

Dad it's pumpkin...It's Marlene

Dad: I'm too weak to talk

Tons of loud noise in the background, almost like white noise, like my dad's engine room, but I thought that was impossible because the phone had to be in the wheelhouse...I still don't know where my dad and Carl took this call.

Me: What's wrong? What do I do?

I can hear Carl talking to me. My dad yelling in the background and tons of static.

Dad: I'm taking on water, call the coast guard. We are 50 miles south of the fort.

Carl tried to give me the GPS coordinates, but I could not understand him and I was shaking so bad that it was difficult for me to write them down on the index cards I had laying by the phone.

I asked Carl several times to repeat, and finally from wherever he was, my dad screamed the coordinates. I wrote them down and still have the paper...2407 North, 8335 West. I grew up in a family of fishermen...all fishermen...Father, both grandfather's, great grandfather's uncles, brother all fishermen. I have no idea what these coordinates mean. I do now.

My mind raced with how to call the coast guard.

I told my dad I loved him and he yelled back: I love you Jamie, I love you Jamie. (Jamie is my younger sister). I just yelled back; I love you dad.

So, I hung up and in the middle of my kitchen, bent over and screamed at the top of my lungs. The emotion almost chokes me as I write this now like it did then.

My mother and son came in from outside, and my husband came over to me. I said dad's sinking I have to call the coast guard.

I remember my mom looking at me, her face worried and sad, as she said, "He's going to lose the Capt. Eddie." like it was a part of our family. I was sad, but relieved that my mom had said that because to me it signified that my dad would be ok. Like she must have known a rescue could happen.

I called my Uncle Wesley back who then told me, my dad had broken down, but was fine. My dad had called his then wife, to call the coast guard. And everything was fine.

But the conversation I had just had with my dad and Carl didn't sound fine. I was screaming into the phone to my uncle, the sweetest calmest man on the planet second only to my Grandpa Potter, that my Dad was not fine, he told me to call the coast guard. I asked my uncle what to do. I gave him my dad's coordinates and he said he was going to call the Coast Guard.

I hung up with my Uncle. My mom started calling everyone she knew still living in the keys and my step dad. My husband went on facebook to try and contact the Coast Guard, because when I called I could not get through.

I racked my brain searching for resources on how to save my dad. The phone call playing over and over again in my mind.

I texted my cousin, who is also from the keys, her dad still lived down there. I told her what was going on and gave her my dad's coordinates.

My mom called my brother, who lives in Port Charlotte, to tell him what was going on. My brother also said he had spoken to my Uncle, who had spoken to my dad's wife and said that yes, my dad broke down, but was fine.

My mom relayed this to me and I picked up the phone and called my dad back because I thought I must be going crazy. This was surreal. Was it happening? Everyone was saying dad was fine, but that is not what I heard.

My dad answered the satellite phone, still screaming. My mom was still on the phone with my brother and walked closer to me so my brother could hear my conversation with my dad. I asked dad clear questions to reconcile the chaos in my mind. I asked:

Me: Dad are you taking on water?

Dad: A very adamant: "Yes" In addition to the yes, my dad said something about a stuffing box. Again, a disappointment to all my fishing ancestors I do not know what this box is, and later when I try to tell people what the problem is, I would only remember the work box.

At this point there were several actions happening in an effort to get to my dad. My cousin called her brother, who called friends that had been anchored up by my dad at Fort Jefferson.

My mom was reaching to her sister in law who's step son was anchored up at Fort Jefferson also. He relayed that he saw my dad leaving the Fort.

I reached out by text, to my ex-marine friend Bonnie who reached out to her friend Kevin, who reached out to his friend in the Coast Guard. This friend, said all helicopters in the area were grounded, but they did get my dad's initial mayday.

My cousin also contacted a Coast Guard friend who was stationed in Key West. The friend put out a mayday and was able to speak to my dad. He also put out a zodiac call to all vessels in the area that my dad's boat was sinking and who could help?

I received a phone number from my cousin for a boat captain with a satellite phone who was in the keys. I called this captain and left a voicemail with my dad's coordinates. I also gave this number to my uncle, because he wanted to get a hold of someone in the keys to get them to go and save my dad. In his calm voice I remember my uncle saying this is a matter of life and death. We'll pay. No price is too large.

My uncle also wanted the number for my mom's sister in law's step son. (I know very confusing), he was also anchored up on Fort Jefferson. However, the captain's parents (my mom's brother and sister in law) did not want the number given out, because they knew their son would try to weather the storm and go save my dad.

At that point I remember not knowing what to tell my uncle. It was like choosing lives. Do we risk one to save one or perhaps lose all? My mom took the phone and spoke to my uncle. I believe my step dad also called my uncle, or my uncle called him to talk about it. I remember hearing my mom say call John, who is my step dad. I still to this day do not know what was said in those conversations.

A third conversation I had with my uncle was the Coast Guard had spoken to my dad, or his wife (I cannot recall), and the Coast Guard was told that my dad had the intake of water under control. My uncle then told me, that the Coast Guard was not going to risk their lives if my dad said he had it under control.

I refuse to believe my dad, told the coast guard he had it under control. From the first time I spoke to my dad at 1:00 PM, he never had it under control, and he knew that.

When I spoke to my dad a third time, it was eerily quiet. Later I would learn that he was on his life raft, and the boat had sunk. His voice was soft and cracked with tears. He kept saying he was so tired, and I told him I knew he was but he had to hang on a little longer because someone was coming to get him. Someone was on their way to get him. I told him I loved him.

At 9:18 that night I sent a text to my sister asking if they were ok? On Sunday at 4:54 PM I received a text back saying *"So far so good? You guys? My dad's wife said she spoke to Carl and they're fine on the boat? How about you guys? Did you stay?"*

At 6:54 I asked Jamie if she had spoken to dad? Then I just asked for her phone number because I did not want to talk to her about dad on text.

When we spoke, she said, *"I actually just heard from dad. His boat is sinking but a cruise ship is coming to get him. He still has insurance on his boat, but man he is going to be in rough shape."*

I relayed my entire story to Jamie. We spoke many times at all hours of the night. She had taken the lead on my dad getting back from the Bahamas, his clothes, money, and his passport. I teased my dad when he returned saying, "Jamie was going to get him back to Florida if she had to swim over and get him herself."

I spoke to Peter on Carnival who told me my dad was fine. He was getting medical attention. I emailed the captain and received a short response that my dad was indeed on the boat. I emailed him wanting confirmation that he was ok. I believe I received that email address from Jamie.

Jamie also told me that Carl didn't make it, because the cruise ship had said there was only one person to rescue. This is also why I sent an email to the cruise ship. I wanted confirmation on the ID of what man they had saved.

I had several emails going with the woman helping my dad get back to the states. She was super nice, but I can't remember her name. I know I purchased his ticket to return. Jamie got his passport to him with some money.

During all this I never spoke to my dad's wife, and Jamie had continuously worked getting my dad back, because I booked his flight, I relayed the return info to my family. My two uncles, who came to Florida and met us at the airport when my dad returned.

On the day my dad returned, I met my sister at the airport and my dad's wife was there, with news crews. It seemed like a lot for someone dealing with such trauma. Too much actually.

With everyone there and the news crews, I was able to see my dad and hug him. However, I did not go back to his house like I planned to make sure he was ok, because there were so many people there and I had no idea where he and his wife stood in their relationship. I'll opt out before I engage in any type of drama. That's just me. I love my dad, but I didn't trust her, and I felt wiped from everything. I just kept playing that first phone call in my head, and wondered if anyone else had heard that from my dad.

The screaming and yelling. Shouting numbers. Me talking to Carl, who was now gone.

It was unreal.

When he arrived, my dad looked weak. Tired. Spent. Dazed. A good friend of his was there and said to me, "I've never seen your dad look like that. We need to get him a wheelchair." So we did.

His wife pushed him out of the airport, amongst reporters. I know they did stop to make statements where my dad thanked Carnival, but I have never watched the interview on TV, nor have I watched the actual rescue sent to me.

I went to my dad's the next day. Visited with him, and my family. We talked about the timeline and tried to put pieces together. At least in my mind I did. I heard reporters had been in the house. Invited by my dad's wife.

Jamie had told me, on the day of my dad's return, reporters had contacted her about showing up at the airport, and Jamie had told them we wanted to keep it private, but I think my dad's wife at the time overruled that decision.

While visiting the house with my dad asleep, his wife wanted to talk to me about us starting over for the sake of my dad. His wife and I had a falling out at the airport.

At that point I thought oh my, my dad is staying with this chic, it was unsettling to say the least, but I thought I needed to make things better so my dad could recover. I agreed on reconciliation, but knew I would never make an attempt to befriend her.

I spent time with my dad who exhausted easily. Especially after talking about the storm.

My sons play hockey and the first time my dad showed up to watch them, after Irma, my oldest son took one look at my dad and started crying as he hugged him.

It's sad to me to think about the Capt. Eddie being gone. I know it's devastating to my dad, but I believe he has made such a huge recovery, and it's nice to have him around more than he's ever been.

We'll still drift into conversations about Carl and why he wouldn't swim out to the life raft. I think my dad tries to answer these questions in his head, but they will never be answered and that has to be tough to live with.

Still, Irma haunts me every now and then. Just this past year, sitting in a trauma training, one of the examples of recognizing your own trauma was an Irma scenario. Where were you? How did you react?

I was working with a partner when I read the scene and questions. I just leaned over and told her I couldn't do the presentation part involving Irma. My throat locked up and my neck hurt from keeping the tears hidden. Later, I had to walk out of the training, just for a second, to get a bit of composure.

Even now, writing this, I had to stop in the middle and just cry.

My husband and I envy my dad's happiness in his simplistic needs. He visits us and we talk about movies, food and it usually ends with me telling him he needs to get on the treadmill more. I'm not sure if he misses the boat. Well, I know he misses the boat, but I'm not sure about the actual job. He keeps himself busy and likes his independence and his freedom and that makes me happy for him. I can imagine sometimes that he misses the feeling on the water, but I often wonder if he's mad at it, for taking away Carl, his boat, his father's wedding band? Especially after giving him so much throughout his life. But when I see my dad, he doesn't seem angry. He seems blessed.

About the Author

Edward Potter, who is now living peacefully with his cats, has seen life in many different shades. He is a single dad of three beautiful children and has a soul of an ancient sailor in him. His fascination for the sea pushed him towards a tragedy in the past but never has he ever given up on his love for nature. Potter still loves nature with all its glory and enjoys going for long walks. With extensive experience on the waves, he has numerous interesting stories to share with the world and feels that now is the right time to do it.

Made in the USA
Las Vegas, NV
08 January 2022